SINGLED OUT
in a
COUPLES WORLD

Christa Smith

Singled Out in a Couples' World

Cover Design by: Sabrina Schlesinger

Reach us on the Internet: www.seanandchristasmith.com

Print ISBN 13 TP: 978-1-7354000-4-4

eBook ISBN 13 eBook: 978-1-7354000-1-3

For Worldwide Distribution, Printed in the United States of America

ENDORSEMENTS

I believe that one of biggest struggles we have in our culture today is contentment—especially with our relationship status (been there!). Christa Smith brings a relatable, practical, and biblical approach to relationships in her book, *Singled Out in a Couples' World.* This book will show you that you don't have to wait around for a relationship to complete you. Instead, you can walk in the fullness of who God has called you to be, regardless of your status.

— Sadie Robertson Huff
Author, Speaker, and Founder of Live Original

Christa Smith is not only a prophetic voice but a prophetic sign of what it means to live wholeheartedly and set apart to the purposes of the kingdom of God. I've had the privilege of serving the body of Christ alongside her and her husband, Sean, in different training settings, and I've witnessed not only the depth in the message but the demonstration of the power of God. Christa lives out the message she carries in a bold and gracious manner and has fruit to back it up! I highly recommend the truths and revelation in these pages as I've seen her ministry transform the lives of many.

—Teofilo Hayashi
Founder Dunamis Movement
Senior Leader of Zion Church, The Send Collab

Christa is an avid communicator and one I have come to know as a friend. To every onlooker, it is obvious that she has satisfied Solomon's question, "Who can find a virtuous woman?" Her book *Singled Out* is not a typical dating book, but rather a firsthand, transparent view of a woman who has walked through the cultural and self-imposed stigmas of singlehood and come out of it realizing that in the journey there are vital muscles that must be developed. Those who let stigmas and cultural expectations circumvent the journey of singlehood come out ill-prepared to face marriage. This book is a masterpiece that reminds us that waiting is not a curse and marriage is not a cure! Christa invites us into both sides of her journey, showing us that God is just as involved in writing our love story as He is in writing our singleness story. I highly recommend this book both for single people who are struggling to enjoy their singleness and married people who fell into the assumption that marriage was the cure.

—Tomi Arayomi
RIG Nation Founder

This is such an important book. As many outside pressures try and convince us that being married is the ultimate goal, Christa takes a rare and fresh approach on the beauty of singleness. This isn't a book on "surviving singleness" but about living your best life in the midst of it. We know Christa personally and she has walked every page of this message out in her personal life. Enjoy her humor, her authenticity, and her biblical approach to living content and full of purpose regardless of your relationship status. It is possible!

—Pastors Dustin & Jamie Bates
Senior Leaders of Church Eleven32

Singled Out is the book I wish I had years ago. Christa's message is steeped in so much wisdom, but it is also witty, funny, relatable, and vulnerable, making you feel like you're chatting with a friend. Her message of singleness goes far beyond relationships and gives us all the tools we need to hold on to any of God's promises while we wait with hopeful expectation.

—Rebecca Bender
Author of Pursuit of Love
Founder of Elevate Academy

If you are single, then you need to read this book. The spiritual intelligence and vulnerability offered by Christa Smith are going to change the way you live your life. I was single until thirty-seven and I know the challenges and even pain that singleness can bring, both personally and in how others relate to you. Although I loved the gift of my extended single years, I wish I had had this book then, because it would have mentored my heart so that I could have really surrendered more to that time of my life and experienced more connection to myself and God and more joy in my journey. This book will take the conflict out of the single life and help you win in your relationship with God, yourself, and others. I recommend you buy it for any Christian friend you know—they will thank you!

—Shawn Bolz
TV Host, Bestselling Author of Translating God, Through the Eyes of Love, *and* Breakthrough Prophecies, Prayers, and Declarations
Podcast Host of the Exploring Series on Charisma Podcast Network

This book is a game-changer for all those tired of playing games with their love lives. Christa brings the power and prophetic edge that she speaks with into this purpose-packed book. This is the book I needed when I was still single. It will shift every reader's perspective on their season, especially if they find themselves single and wanting more. We are encouraged and reminded through Christa's words that our relationship status should not box in our lives, but rather be an opportunity to walk with God on the sweetest adventure. Christa is not here to play, and we desperately need the truth she shares. Her story will challenge you and champion you in the pursuit of everything God has for you.

—Jenny Erlingsson
Missions in Iceland, Speaker & Author
Milk & Honey in the Land of Fire & Ice *and* Becoming His

I thank God for voices in the body of Christ like Christa Smith! I have the privilege of knowing her closely and attesting to her character and her devoted life to Christ. Not only does she flow in a powerful prophetic anointing, she also communicates truth in a simple but masterful way. I deeply encourage you to dive into this reading, as I am positive that the message Christa carries will impact you, reveal the heart and the mind of God in a transforming manner, and offer you fresh perspectives of the God-given calling on your life.

—Junia Hayashi
Senior Leader Zion Church
Dunamis Movement

The first time I met Christa I was impacted by her sparkly blue eyes, sense of fun, and passionate love for Jesus. This book allows you to meet this authentic Christa as she unpacks this tricky subject of singleness in a transparent but courageous style. Christa understands the humiliation and pressure of the world of "singleness" often experienced in the church, but she manages to instruct us on how to navigate this path with grace and faith. This book is a captivating read, full of great stories, impactful choices, and amazing honesty. I believe we need to understand our amazing young men and women called to pursue God, without making them feel they need to apologize for still being single. Read and enjoy!

—Rachel Hickson
Heartcry for Change
Oxford, England

I am so grateful that Christa decided to write *Singled Out in a Couples' World*. This book is so needed in the world right now. Without a shadow of a doubt, I believe this book will help many to not grow weary in their season of actively preparing and waiting for their future spouse. Christa's transparency and commitment to Jesus is apparent on each page. I love that within her journey of waiting she chose to "lean in" to God's word and promises over her life. Her love for God and the beautiful story He wrote for her life is a testament to what is possible when we trust God with every area of our lives!

—Natasha Miller
Co-Founder of One University

I got saved when I was eighteen and was engaged at twenty-one. We had our first daughter when I was twenty-five and now we have four children. I am only thirty-four years old. When Christa sent me *Singled Out*, I was excited that she had completed her first book, but to be honest, I wondered how I would be able to relate to the content. Well, I just finished reading and I want to say this book is for everyone, and it is *exploding* with hope. Our life on earth is short in light of eternity, but this life is a journey of learning to TRUST GOD. It is impossible to please God without faith. With this easy read, Christa imparts wisdom that will encourage all of us God lovers in the journey of life, the journey of faith. One benefit of being in the family of God is that we have the opportunity to learn from each other's friendship with God. God shares His heart secrets with His friends and Christa is a true friend of God. If you've realized that you're in process like the rest of us, then you want to read *Singled Out*.

—Riche Seltzer
Evangelist, Founder of Revivalist Culture

Christa Smith's book *Singled Out In A Couples' World* will bring hope to those singles who may feel forgotten. The daydream of the storybook wedding and the arrival of a Prince Charming is most women's dream. Because the promise of marriage appears to be delayed, one can become hopeless and even desperate to "make IT happen." I've personally experienced the ministry of this powerful woman and I know that you will be inspired to believe! As she walked me through her life's testimony, it became clear to me that Christa had been given a timely word to shift the reader's perspective. Get ready to be challenged and changed. I will leave you with one of my favorite quotes from the book: "When we maintain confidence and assurance that God is for us and loves us, we can be at peace knowing He will release His blessings at the right time for everyone that is involved in the situation. Remember, your marriage is bigger than just you!"

—Yolanda Stith, *God's Friend*
Lead Pastor at ANWA Baltimore
Host of Junia's Table Live with Yolanda Stith
Author of Invisible Battlegrounds *and* Jael's Tent

Singled Out In A Couples' World is a much-anticipated and needed book. Christa Smith is a dear friend with whom I have shared a similar single-to-married journey, so it is even more personal to me. I have rarely met a woman who has walked out her years of singleness with the health, honesty, humor, and grace Christa has. It is so helpful for singles to hear from someone who is actually speaking from relatable experience with real authority and not just opinion. This book will take single Christians on a real journey into embracing their season of singleness and getting the fullness of what God has for you, without losing the hope for marriage. I really believe this book is a first of its kind and will bring perspective, healing, and hope for the many who read it. *Singled Out In A Couples' World* is an incredible resource to the single body of Christ.

—Amy Ward
Youth With A Mission

Singled Out in a Couples' World is a myth-buster and game-changer, a deviation from the status quo. This is exactly what we need on such an important topic as singleness. Christa's story and insights are remarkable because she has lived it and has decided to put it in print. It's natural to assume this book is for singles, but it is actually important for all to grasp the messages within these pages. It is an excellent book and I can't wait till you read it.

—Eric Johnson
Pastor, Speaker, and Author
Bethel Church

Christa Smith has honed into the heart of a single with love, insight, and compassion. She can do so because she walked out single life in purity and holiness. If you are single, you will laugh, cry, and sigh with her true-to-life stories of both the joys and struggles of living out the single life with victory, and a good dose of a healthy sense of humor.

—Cindy Jacobs
Generals International

ACKNOWLEDGEMENTS

Kathleen Harwell and Lauri Inman: Thanks for being the best big sisters and always encouraging me in my unique journey and adding so much humor along the way! Love you both!

Cherie Bolz and Lauren Lancaster: Thanks for always having my back and even flying up to be a part of the photoshoot for this book cover! Everywhere you girls are is an instant God party! We have the most incredible friendship and I thank God for that because He was the One who brought us all together all those years ago! And Lauren, you killed it on my makeup—thank you!

Cheena Kumar: Girl, you're amazing! Thank you for the hours of editing you gave me! Your feedback was invaluable! Your friendship has been such a gift in my life. Not only have we walked side by side for the last eighteen years, you walked this book out with me! Thank you for always praying for me, encouraging me, and believing in me!

Jenny Erlingsson: My book coach! Thank you for being willing to come alongside me for this project! I knew I needed you to help me finish this book! Thank you for extending me grace in the busy seasons, yet always reminding me of the end result! Grateful for both your friendship and support—thank you again for believing my story needed to be shared!

Rachel Heisel: Thank you for capturing exactly what I was envisioning with the photography! You are such a talent, so gifted, and incredibly creative! Thank you for sharing your gift with me!

Allison Armerding: Thank you for saying "yes" to this project in the midst of your already busy schedule! So grateful for your insight and light-handed editing—you brought the final refining this project needed!

Sabrina Schlesinger: Sis, thank you for doing such a great job designing my book cover! To have a friend be part of this project was such a gift. Thank you for your constant patience and grace as this project took way longer than expected!

DEDICATION

I first and foremost dedicate this book to my parents. We all know this book wouldn't exist if I didn't have you two as parents. I'm convinced God gave me the best of the best. He knew I needed you two as my mom and dad. Thank you for never putting pressure on me to conform to the timelines of society, but rather always encouraging me to fully run after Jesus, no matter the cost and no matter what anyone else thought! Your unrelenting prayers and support were the earthly assurance I needed to walk this journey out. Being your daughter has been one of my greatest joys. Thanks for showing me what family is—unconditional and unwavering!

Secondly, I want to dedicate this book to my husband, Sean, the love of my life. Without you, the second part of my story wouldn't have been written! I've told you a hundred times, and I'll tell you a hundred more, "I waited twenty years for you, but I would have waited twenty more!" With every fiber of my being, I love you. I believe our stories were always meant to be intertwined. I lovingly call you "my reward" because I get the privilege of being your wife, making all the waiting worth it! God gives the best gifts and I am daily reminded of that truth being married to you.

CONTENTS

FOREWORD

I sat there, stunned.

Everything Christa was saying hit my heart in a way I longed for twenty-year-old me to have felt. I knew her story would change the lives of those navigating the journey of singleness, with all its highs and lows. At that moment, my own story of singleness found redemption, beyond just finding my husband. Christa gave a kind of clarity and hope seldom heard in the messaging around me. I clasped on to every word, story, and revelation she shared, knowing how important they would be for another single heart desperate to find optimism. My prayer was that her words would soon, one day, be put into a book.

Now that prayer is answered. It is a privilege to declare to you that you, too, will find healing and purpose in the chapters you are about to read.

You see, I've been there, too. My friends' lives were moving on at what felt like the speed of light, and there I was, twenty-six, single as ever, parents as roommates, working an unfulfilling 9-to-5 job to make ends meet. For me, exciting events consisted of weekend weddings, bridal and baby showers, and college graduations. Everywhere I turned, someone was taking their next big step except me. Can you relate? I remember thinking, I can't go to one more wedding! I had been a bridesmaid sixteen times. Yes, sixteen. I had this ache in my heart to find that someone. What in the world was I doing wrong? Why wasn't I attracting the things I wanted most? Was I ugly? Boring? Behind schedule?

I couldn't figure it out. But the secret I learned in that season of life is something Christa highlights beautifully: It just wasn't time yet.

Now, don't close the book already. I know you've heard that said time and time before, so much so that I'm sure your hand clenched at the sight of the phrase. The topic of singleness and waiting is not popular in today's culture. We worship sex. We compromise healthy relationships for quick fixes. Some believe the narrative of singleness is not only dull but terrifying. They fill in the blanks of their lives, assuming they'll miss out or lack something inside themselves.

One of the most significant lies of the enemy over your life is that you are running out of time. Today is the day to shut down this self-imposed mental clock that taunts you at every birthday, baby shower, and bridesmaid speech, saying, "Time is almost up." The narrative of our Heavenly Father is different. He says, "I am not bound by time! I am the Creator of time, yet exist outside of it. I have not forgotten you or the dreams in your heart. Trust me with the timing of your life."

We do not surrender our hopes and dreams to a God who does not care. We do surrender our control and fears to a God who replaces them with peace, trust, and security in Him.

This offering to God doesn't come easy, and I won't give you a cheap, feel-good answer that it will. I wish I had someone like Christa to share her story with me as I was asking myself the hard questions and becoming honest about my doubts. In these pages, Christa will speak directly to the ache in your heart. You will no longer feel alone as she becomes your guide. She will give you support and courage for your process while providing a divine and timely perspective on this vulnerable topic.

Your time is not up.

You have not missed the mark.

Begin, perhaps again, to see singleness as a timely gift.

Begin, perhaps again, to trust God with the timing of your life.

—Havilah Cunnington
Author and Founder of Truth to Table

INTRODUCTION

I'm so glad you decided to read this book! I want to officially welcome you to a journey of discovery and conversation about walking out singleness as a follower of Jesus. My hope in writing this book is not simply to share my personal journey, but to encourage many of you who are walking out this same journey. I once heard a statistic that the majority of the people sitting in church are single, and that they are one of the least addressed groups within the church. I think it's time we change that, don't you?

The topic of singleness isn't typically addressed from the pulpit, unless it's that awkward invitation of, "If you're single and are believing for a spouse, please stand." Listen, can we please not do that to single people anymore? And all the single people said, "Amen!"

I do not want to approach this conversation with the goal of just helping you get through this part of your life until you get married. Rather, my desire is that by reading this book, you will gain the tools needed to be content in your singleness, whether you get married or not.

In this book, I want to go beyond the surface of the typical conversations you may have found yourself in as a single person. I want to go after your heart. Being single can actually be a gift when we choose to change how we view it.

So, before you read this book, can I ask two things of you?

First, will you open your heart to receive what may be a new perspective on your singleness? If you find yourself with any skepticism about being single, I'd like to ask you to trust this process. Because maybe, just maybe, you are holding this book in your hands for a reason.

Two, please don't read this book for someone else. Read this for yourself. Often, we get information or hear a message and automatically assume it's for other people. Many times it's more comfortable to hear it for someone else than to address and deal with things that are being challenged in our own life.

I don't claim to have all the answers, but I am someone who has walked a similar journey and cares about you. You are not alone. God has you, even when it doesn't feel like it. I promise you He does. So, take a deep breath, exhale, and let's get reading! I believe the Lord has something great for you!

For His Glory,
Christa

NEVER WOULD HAVE CALLED IT

Let me introduce myself.

1. My name is Christa Smith.
2. I didn't fall in love till I was thirty-eight years old.
3. I got married when I was thirty-nine years old. (Three months before I turned forty!)
4. Prior to dating my husband, I had never been in a long-term relationship or been in love.
5. I was the girl who was always the bridesmaid and never the bride. I've actually been asked to be a bridesmaid *thirteen* times.
6. In fact, I've probably been involved in over twenty weddings (as a bridesmaid, officiant, blessing-prayer, guest book attendant, etc.). And that's a conservative number.

7. Watching the movie *27 Dresses* was a bit too close to home, I do have to say.

8. Being the third wheel was my norm.

9. My friends continually scanned the baptism tank for possible suitors to hook me up with. They'd say, "Hey, he's saved." My response: "He's only been clean for twenty-four hours."

10. I have lost count of all the awkward church match-making moments where my singleness was put on full blast and I was advertised as if I was for sale. The actual verbiage used one time was (and I quote), "Applications are available in the front lobby if you'd like to pursue her." This was said in front of a thousand people, and the event was being live-streamed. I'm not kidding.

11. I've probably had a half-dozen men tell me that God told them I was their wife within my first conversation with them.

SELAH. Let that sink in.

All this to say, I get singleness. I understand process and waiting on God to answer your prayers. As you might guess, my story of singleness is a little different than most of the ones you may have heard.

I don't know about you, but throughout my life I have often found myself saying these words: "Wow, I would have never called that!" So many times, things turned out way differently than I expected them to. Being single at thirty-eight years old was certainly not what I thought my life would look like at that age. My expectation was that at thirty-eight I would be well into a marriage and mom life with kids. But that wasn't at all how it turned out.

It felt like every natural milestone that others were experiencing seemed to be passing me by:

➤ **Meet that someone special in your twenties. Check.**

➤ **Get married in your twenties. Check.**

➤ **First baby in your twenties or early thirties. Check.**

➤ **Second baby in your late twenties or thirties. Check.**

By the time most of the people around me were checking their fourth box, I wasn't even close to checking my first! I often found myself saying, "Hello, Jesus! Do you remember me? It's me, Christa! Yes, that's me waving my hands in the air, sending up an SOS signal! Everyone around me seems to be progressing forward and checking off all of their relational boxes. What about me?"

I never expected to be single for that long. I thought for sure that falling in love and getting married would happen sooner for me. I dated some guys short-term in high school and then during one summer of college. In my twenties, and once in my thirties, I went on some dates, but that was it. I basically wasn't in a significant relationship from the age of nineteen on. If you do the math, that means I wasn't in a relationship for nineteen years. *Nineteen* years. Yes, you read that right.

Like so many people, I wanted to be in a significant,

love-centered relationship that allowed me to share my life with another person. I was captivated by the thought of giving my heart to someone fully and sharing the daily moments of our lives. I wanted the front-row seat to all the big and small moments, cheering each other on as we moved forward together in life.

Instead, any guy I was interested in quickly put me in the friend zone. Many of these guys told me that I was the type of girl they would marry, but for the moment they just wanted to date around and have fun. Translation: They wanted to party and have sex. These guys knew I loved Jesus with my heart and body, and sex was never going to happen with me before marriage. Therefore, the friend zone became my norm.

On the other hand, when guys did pursue me, I never had real feelings for them. I longed for a connection, a spark of chemistry, but I didn't find it. So, I waited. I wasn't interested in dating just for the sake of dating. Being casual with my heart has never been my style, nor was I interested in being casual with someone else's heart. I knew the way I was wired—once I gave my heart away, I would be all in. So giving it to just anyone wasn't an option. I knew I had to be intentional and selective about who I would be in a relationship with.

Because of this, I felt like I was so delayed and falling behind everyone around me. Honestly, I think that appears to be true in many areas of our lives, especially if we judge them based on society's timelines and expectations. I learned through the process of waiting that our lives are a continual journey with the Lord. We have to be content with the timeline

He has us on and we can't compare the timelines of our lives with someone else's.

Even my siblings and I all have very different stories from one another when it comes to our romantic relationships. I am the youngest of three girls. My middle sister got married during her college years at twenty-two years old. My oldest sister didn't get married until she was thirty-one years old. Each of us married great men and are all serving the Lord with our spouses, yet our timelines were very different.

This confirms that there is no formula to how life is supposed to go. You just have to walk out *your* story with the Lord and be patient with the journey He takes you on. If you know who the Author of your story is, then there is peace that comes in knowing that He is leading you to good places and has wonderful things in store for you. The Lord desires a deep and intimate relationship with you, and because of this I believe He allows times of waiting to deepen our dependence and intimacy with Him, especially in matters of the heart. The Lord wants us to have His best, and oftentimes that requires waiting.

The Process of Preparation

Because there are two people in the equation of marriage, there is often a process of maturing and preparation that *each* person needs to go through. Sometimes, we may be waiting because there are areas of healing that need to take place in our personal lives. Other times, we may still be waiting because the person the Lord is preparing for us needs to go through the process that the Lord has for them. Trusting the timing of the Lord is so essential, and yet so often misunderstood. It's easy to quickly jump to conclusions and misunderstand the heart of the Lord when we are in seasons of waiting. If we don't understand how deeply the Lord loves us, then our view of waiting can easily become distorted. We feel forgotten, rejected, or maybe abandoned because things aren't happening as we have prayed or believed they would. We find ourselves believing that a delay means He doesn't love us or care about us. But, if we truly understand what He did for us on the cross, that Jesus sacrificially gave His life for us and Father God intentionally gave His only Son for us, we will realize that there is no greater act or display of love that can be shown. We are *so* loved and cherished by the Lord:

> *For God **so loved** the world that He gave His only begotten Son, that whoever believes in Him should not perish but have everlasting life.* (John 3:16 NKJV, emphasis added)

The Lord doesn't just love you—He *so loves* you. He is all in, holding nothing back from us. It's like when someone says to you that they aren't just single, they are *so* single. In other words, there are no options! They are not dating, and they have zero prospects! Take that concept and apply it to the love of God. He so loves *you*, which means He is madly in love with you, and because of His deep love for you He gave His only

Son! That is an incomprehensible kind of love! His desire for you is to experience the full depth of it! If you find yourself in a season of waiting, it isn't because you are forgotten, rejected, or abandoned. It's because God is preparing you for an incredible gift, a blessing that is fueled by His love for you!

Good things often take time. The Lord wants us to be in a place where we can enjoy what He has been preparing for us and fully appreciate it when we receive it! There are times in my life when I have looked back and understood why the Lord had me wait. I needed that time to mature, to heal, to have my heart opened. I had to have an encounter with Him that changed my perspective before I received the blessing He wanted to give me. I needed healing in my heart so I would carefully nurture what would be given to me. *Waiting is not a curse. It is actually the invitation to trust God beyond your current capacity.* Waiting is stretching. It's hard, but when we look back over various situations in our lives, we can see, with greater clarity, the purpose of our waiting.

A Complicated and Beautiful Journey

Growing up, my family didn't have a lot of extra money, but it always seemed like we had what we needed. My parents were both teachers, and as you know, teachers are some of the most underpaid, hardest-working people around. One bonus to them both being teachers, however, was that we had summers off together as a family. These times in my childhood were filled with camping vacations and road trips for weeks on end.

My parents made a lot of sacrifices to give me and my sisters a stable and loving home. One of the sacrifices they made was my mom also chose to put her teaching career on hold until my two older sisters and I were all in school full-time, which meant that the five of us lived off my dad's teaching salary for several years. Because of this decision, I always had what I needed, but maybe not the extra things I saw my friends getting—for example, a car.

When each of us girls turned sixteen, we were allowed to use the family car—a brown Volkswagen bus. But when I went away to college, I didn't have enough money for school and a car, so I chose to keep my debt to a minimum and go without one. You make sacrifices when you understand the priority of the moment. My priority during college was to get the best education I could, go fully after God, and walk away with as little debt as possible. My parents sacrificed and generously contributed to my education costs, and I took full credit loads every term. I also worked a part-time job and was a resident assistant, which gave me free room and board. It wasn't always easy or convenient, but I understood what was important during that season and a car wasn't at the top of the list.

So, imagine my excitement when I graduated and my dad gave me one of the family cars! Wheels meant freedom—finally—as well as reliable transportation to my first full-time job. Unfortunately, however, a few months later, the engine blew. I knew it was time for me to make my first major purchase. I ended up finding a great deal on a cherry-red, two-door sports car with electric windows and air conditioning. After the

Volkswagen bus, I thought AC and electric windows were super fancy. I loved that car and took impeccable care of it. I made sure to do all the maintenance on time and never skimped on what needed to be serviced.

One day, a co-worker made a comment to me as we were walking into the office. "You really love that car. You take such great care of it."

"If you knew how long I went without a car, then you would know why I am taking such great care of it!" I responded. "I know what life was like without it!"

I've seen this truth play out again and again in my own life. If there has been a long wait for something to come to pass, my gratitude increases when that prayer is answered and breakthrough comes. This has certainly been my experience in my marriage with Sean. I lived so many years single, and my single years were good and fulfilling. But Sean adds so much to my life now. Being married to him has been my greatest joy. Truly. We both know what life was like before we had one another, so we enjoy it so much more with each other. We waited for each other and now we savor one another. In our relationship, Sean and I don't get caught up in the little things that could ultimately cause division. We focus on the constant goodness and kindness of the Lord in bringing us together. I am so grateful and appreciative for the gift he is to me.

The process you go through when you are waiting for an answer to prayer produces gratitude in you when the Lord brings that gift into your life. If you are too familiar with something and it's just "normal" to you, you won't give the gift as much value, think too much of it, or take the best care of it. You will do only what's needed without fully appreciating what you receive since you don't realize what life was like without it. But when you have the awareness of what life was like before your answered prayer, you will be all the more grateful and appreciative when you meet the one you've been waiting for. You will be more intentional about stewarding and nurturing your relationship well.

When we maintain confidence and assurance that God is for us and loves us, we can be at peace, knowing He will release His blessings at the right time for *everyone* involved in the situation. Remember, your marriage is bigger than just you! There is another person who has a part to play in this beautiful promise, and the Lord wants both of you to experience the fullness of what He has in store!

Although I felt very delayed in my life concerning marriage and family, I knew I hadn't missed it. I believe I was smack dab in the middle of God's will for my life regardless of my relationship status. I didn't always understand the delays, but I knew God was for me and that He loved me. Therefore, I was ultimately confident that He would work everything out. I just needed to trust Him on the journey.

The journey part can't be underestimated. I didn't want to rush God's timeline, nor did I want to lower my expectations and just make someone work. I wanted God to write my love story, no matter the time it took. He had written all the other parts of my life. I knew this would be no different. I believe we all have to come to the realization that God really does write the best stories. If you don't believe that, then it's really difficult to wait on His timing and lean into His process. We must have deep assurance that God will come through and that the wait will be worth it. But I also want to paint an accurate picture. It's really easy to say these things, but it was another thing to walk it out for nineteen years. The longer the timeline, the harder it is to trust. And the longer you try to trust, the harder it is to keep your hope alive. Believe me, I get it, because I had to walk it out!

Each of us must come to the place where we accept our lives for the journeys that they are. Journeys can be easy, hard, fun, mundane, boring, unpredictable, exciting, surprising, complicated, painful, hilarious, growing, confusing, purposeful, disappointing, fulfilling, and life-changing! Life can be wonderful and at the same time, not at all what you expect. The journey is layered, complicated, and beautiful. Walking the journey of singleness is no different. *It is layered, complicated, and beautiful.* Be encouraged that you are not doing this alone. You have a Savior and Friend named Jesus who is with you every step of the way. I am also so honored to take this journey with you and to encourage you in it.

ZERO IN ON:

➤ **Waiting is not a curse. It is actually the invitation to trust God beyond your current capacity.**

➤ Things don't always turn out like you expect, but that doesn't mean they aren't good!

➤ The process you go through when you are waiting for answered prayers produces gratitude in you when the Lord brings that gift into your life.

02

THE BIG ASK

The summer break between my freshmen and sophomore years of college set me up for a life-changing moment. I went home during this time and ended up reconnecting with, and soon dating, a guy with whom I had gone to high school. He was a year older and in a different class, so I hadn't known him very well in high school, but I knew he was naturally cool and really handsome with a kind soul.

Apparently, in the years before we met up again, this guy had made some decisions he wasn't proud of, and experienced a lot of shame and brokenness because of it. Much of our relationship revolved around me trying to prove his worth to him and show him how valuable and special he was. It never seemed to penetrate his perspective. Every time I tried to gently encourage him, he argued with me, not believing he had worth or value. I remember wanting so badly for him to experience freedom and for shame to be defeated in his life. I told him that God had already forgiven him—he just needed to forgive himself. But he not only couldn't do that—he could not even seem to wrap his mind around that concept. The enemy had filled him with so much shame that he truly didn't believe he was worthy to be forgiven. He didn't believe God could love him because of those past decisions. He lived in a constant state of self-sabotage, which led him to use drugs and cheat on me.

I found out after we broke up that he had been living a double life the majority of our relationship. I was completely unaware that any of that had been going on, but I did know something wasn't right. His behavior was erratic and unpredictable. He would disappear for a couple of days at a time with no communication and no explanation. When he suddenly reappeared, he always had an excuse, and I always wanted to believe it. He would claim some emergency had come up or his cell phone was dead because he forgot to charge it.

All the signs were there, but I just didn't want to read them. *Isn't it funny how people will often tell us who they are, but we don't believe them or take them seriously?* He always said to me, "I don't deserve you, Christa. I know I'm going to mess this up and you aren't going to want to be with me anymore." Not only was he telling me what he believed about himself, he was also subconsciously telling me what was about to happen. But I didn't believe him. I didn't want to believe him. I thought I could nurture him into wholeness. I thought I could pep talk him into his freedom. But the truth is, you can't heal or restore someone who doesn't want to be healed or restored. He wasn't willing to look in the mirror and take ownership of his stuff. He didn't want to deal with his baggage, and because of that, just as he predicted, he sabotaged everything we had because shame set the narrative of his identity.

Days after the truth about the drugs and cheating came out, I returned to school to begin my sophomore year of college, only to learn that the guy I had had a major crush on for the entirety of my freshmen year had started dating a friend of mine over the summer. This friend just so happened to be assigned to live across the hall from me. I remember moving back into the dorms, finding out this "amazing" news, and immediately going on a long walk to get off campus and cry. I had liked this guy my entire freshmen year, but he was never interested in me, which was really disappointing. Then I had gone home for the summer and dated the guy from high school who ended up cheating on me and lying to me for the majority of our short relationship, only to return to college and find that my crush who rejected me was dating the girl across the hall! Lord, You have got to be kidding me!

During that walk, I prayed one of the most life-changing prayers I had ever spoken. I said, "Jesus, I give You my heart. Guard it, shield it, and give it back to me when You want me to give it away." It was a simple and slightly cheesy prayer, but I meant every single word, and deep peace came over me after I prayed it. The heaviness I had carried a few moments before lifted. I felt deep assurance that the Lord had me, and the only thing I needed to focus on was leaning into Him every day. He would get me through.

As the school year went on, each day got easier. As I watched my ex-crush take the girl across the hall on dates and bring her flowers, I just leaned deeper into the Lord and it hurt less and less. I reminded myself often that I wanted God's best for me, and if it wasn't this guy (I thought he was wonderful) then the man the Lord had for me must be amazing. Nineteen years later, I would find out that it was a hundred percent true.

This didn't happen overnight. I had to commit myself to walk out this prayer by giving every part of me over to God *every* day.

Daily, I had to make the choice to trust God with the dreams and desires of my heart.

Daily, I had to root myself in who He was and not let my feelings and emotions overtake me.

Daily, I had to be intentional about being grateful for what I did have in my life, and not focus on what I didn't have.

Daily, I had to choose not to compare myself to all the other girls meeting their future husbands and getting engaged and married.

Daily, I had to choose to trust that the Lord had me on the path I was supposed to be on.

Every day I was presented with the choice to trust God.

Even though I knew I was right where the Lord wanted me to be, my path looked so different from everyone around me. This was about our walk together, just me and the Lord. I had to make the choice not to run ahead, but to stay beside Him, holding His hand and keeping in stride with His every step.

When I prayed that prayer at nineteen years old, I felt like I stepped into a unique place of grace with my single-ness. I truly believe God's grace rested on me because I chose to abide in trusting Him. Trusting Him with my dreams and desires released a rest in me. It removed the feelings driving me to make something happen and allowed me to trust that He had ordained my steps, and therefore, I would not miss His plans for me:

> *The Lord directs the steps of the godly. He delights in every detail of their lives.* (Psalm 37:23 NLT)

I found myself becoming really comfortable with being single, and for the most part, it felt like a non-issue. Being the third or fifth wheel didn't bother me. I did have an occasional cry here or there when the desire to be married felt like a far-off dream. Like the times I was a bridesmaid for one of the thirteen weddings I was in. Or when my birthday arrived and I was reminded that another year had passed in which I was still waiting. I would have my cry, and then regroup, refocus, and step back into the Lord's covering of grace. This pattern repeated until many years later, when the Lord took this journey to another level.

The Question

I remember it clearly. It was my thirty-fifth birthday, and like most birthdays in my adult years, I blew out my candles making the same wish: "This is the year I am going to meet my husband, in Jesus' Name!" But that year, as I blew out those candles, it was as though I blew the grace I had been living in right out of me! Something inside me changed that day. I don't know if I can even describe it. Feelings and emotions I had never experienced swelled up inside me. I felt restless, lonely, and discontent with my singleness. The grace I had been walking in since I was nineteen years old was nowhere to be found. I suddenly found myself viewing my relationship status through a different filter, a skewed lens, if you will. I felt so unsettled.

I've often wondered why the Lord allowed those emotions to erupt in me at that moment, and I've since concluded He allowed me to experience the depth of my longing to be married so that later, when He asked me a specific question, I would be able to fully grasp what He was asking for. He didn't lift the grace to be cruel or unkind—it was actually quite the opposite. He lifted it to expose the depth of my desire, so I could understand the depth of what He was asking me. He wanted me to be fully honest and specific in my answer to His question, and therefore, the grace had to be removed.

These new emotions and feelings lasted several weeks, until one day I heard Him ask me something that forever changed my walk with Him: "Christa, if you never get married, will I be enough?"

I couldn't believe what He was asking me. What could He possibly mean if I *never got married*, was *He enough*?

Ummm, no You are not enough, was my first thought. My second thought was, *You better not be calling me to be celibate. Seriously, I do not want to be the forty-year-old virgin, God!*

But then He asked again. "Christa, if you never get married, *am I enough?*"

This time the question came with a weight to it. I felt the seriousness of what He was asking me. So I let the words sink in. I let them soak into my heart, my emotions, my spirit, and my body. Every part of me felt the weight and the cost of what He was asking me. I reflected on my life and thought of all the times I had been on my face crying out to the Lord, asking Him to use me to bring Him glory! So many times, I chose to follow Him and go against the status quo. I had made so many choices to give Him all of me, holding nothing back. I knew I had to choose to believe that He was enough, but if I'm honest, in that moment, He wasn't. I wanted a husband and children. I knew I was created to build family and create a beautiful life with another person. But I felt the Lord asking for all of it. He was asking for the husband, the marriage, the dream, my idea of family, my fantasy of my future, my definition of fulfillment and happiness. He was asking if He could write my story instead of me. He was giving me the choice to trust Him, but to trust Him in that way, it required me to surrender at another level.

I knew this decision could cost me a price I didn't even fully understand at that moment. I could feel the weight of my destiny in this decision, and I knew what I decided that day would affect the rest of my life. This was about the relationship between Him and me, between Father and daughter. This was about my legacy. It was the Father asking His daughter, "*Am I enough?*"

I got on my face and wept before the Lord. I weighed the cost of what He was asking, and after much contemplation I answered Him with this: "You're not, but I want You to be." That was a hundred percent how I felt. In that moment, He didn't feel like enough for me. But I knew that if I wanted true happiness, if I wanted the life I had always prayed for and to live out the destiny of the Lord, this was a defining moment.

As soon as I answered Him, I felt a wave of peace wash over me. The grace that had been gone for the previous few weeks suddenly returned. I immediately knew I was resting in the pleasure of the Father, and regardless of the end result, I knew He had me. It was in that surrender and knowing that I found my peace again.

The next year and a half didn't go as I expected. I thought I would just live in the bubble of grace that washed over me when I gave Him my answer. Instead, the next eighteen months brought the hard reality of walking out my decision. The Lord was asking me to surrender *everything*. He showed me a vision of me holding the dream of getting married, coming to an altar before Him, and laying that dream at His feet. Whenever I saw this vision of me putting that dream down before Him, I always saw Him putting His hand on top of my head. It was Him showing me we were going to walk this out together, that I was not alone in the process.

Grieving the Loss of the Dream

When the Lord asked me if He was enough for me, I knew He

wanted me to lay the desire of marriage down before Him. But when you lay something down, there is no promise that you will get it back. I had to lay this desire at the feet of the Lord, not knowing if I was going to get married. I had to trust Him with the end result no matter what happened. Because I was laying something down I didn't know I would get back, I grieved it like any other loss. I mourned the loss of the dream, the loss of my desire for marriage and partnership. I ached over the possibility that I would never build the family I always thought I would have. I let go of what I thought would bring me my ultimate happiness and fulfillment, which was marriage.

Grieving is a natural process when something is given up, lost, or dies. The grieving process has five stages:

1. Denial
2. Anger
3. Bargaining
4. Depression
5. Acceptance[1]

What people don't tell you is that those five stages ebb and flow. They don't go through a clean and tidy linear process where you start at stage one, and then when that is finished you go straight to stage two. All the stages collide into one another, intertwine, and surface at the most inconvenient and unexpected moments. If you've gone through a grieving process before, then you know what I am talking about. There were times I would be in public, have a wave of grief hit me,

---

1 Elisabeth Kübler-Ross and David Kessler, *On Grief and Grieving: Finding the Meaning of Grief Through the Five Stages of Loss*. (New York, Toronto: Scribner, 2005).

and feel like bursting into tears. I would have to think happy thoughts until the swell of emotion passed over. There were days during that season when I would wake up heavy and sad with feelings of discouragement threatening to rob me of the amazing day that awaited me. This was not normal. My typical mood in the morning is happy and excited to take on my day! I am a morning person, so I remember having to make a choice in those moments to not get on the "depression" train or the "pity party" train. You fill in the blank and there is a train waiting for you to hop right on!

For the next year and a half, I had to make intentional choices to stay in a place of peace and joy, trusting that the Lord was the One who initiated this whole process. He was the One who had asked me the question. He was the One who invited me into this journey of deeper surrender to Him. Therefore, I knew He was leading me from a place of love, like a good Father does. I knew that no matter what I felt, I could trust Him. He was faithful as He walked with me. I wasn't alone, even though the enemy wanted me to believe I was. The enemy tried to convince me that God didn't have anything good in store for me. He wanted me to agree with the lie that the plans God had for me were to harm me and *not* to prosper me. But I knew what Jeremiah 29:11 (NKJV) said:

> *For I know the thoughts that I think toward you, says the Lord, thoughts of peace and not of evil, to give you a future and a hope.*

I knew the plans the Lord had for me. I knew they were good. I knew with Him I *did* have hope and a future of promise! Deuteronomy 31:6 (NLT) also says this:

> *So be strong and courageous! Do not be afraid and do not panic before them. For the Lord your God will personally go ahead of you. He will neither fail you nor abandon you.*

I knew these truths and so many more. If we know who God is, then even when we find ourselves in unfamiliar, foreign places, there is a peace we can abide in because His Spirit abides in us. We tap into a greater place of trust the deeper we surrender.

The entire question the Lord asked me was three little words, *"Am I enough?"* He wanted to remove any and all conditions within me that were required for my happiness. He wanted to take my versions of happiness that were circumstance-based and make them God-based. He was asking me to be all in, holding nothing back, fully living for Him. And the truth is, the deeper I surrendered, the greater the peace I experienced.

Is He Enough for You?

The grieving process ebbed and flowed for about eighteen months, and then there came a point when it felt like it had run its course and the grace fully returned. I felt like myself again. I woke up with excitement for life! I felt fulfilled and was fully at peace with the very real possibility that I may not get married. I was actually okay with it. I had wonderful relationships with my family and friends, and I felt really content. At that time, I had been pastoring for over ten years, preaching regularly, and living out who I was called to be. I decided that if the Lord could use me more as a single person, then it was worth it to me. I wanted my life to give Him glory. I wanted my life to be one of the many rewards Jesus would get for His suffering on the cross. He gave His life for me. I wanted to give Him all of mine.

I believe every follower of Christ must go through this process. We have to learn how to trust Him with every aspect of our life, not just parts of it. As a single person, I totally understand how difficult it is for this question to be received, but it must be asked.

I want you to take a moment and ask yourself the same question the Lord asked me. "If I never get married, is He enough?" Don't answer right away. Allow the weight of the question to penetrate you. It's okay if fear, panic, and anger surface. It's all a part of the process. In this season of your life, the Lord is asking you *if He is enough*. This is such an important question to answer because it is one that will be presented multiple times to you throughout your life. How you answer determines so much. This is a question that not only needs to be asked in relation to your singleness but in every area of your life.

The Lord is so intentional with His kids, and His ways are not our ways. Because of that, we often find ourselves waiting for different things. Right now in your life, if you are single, maybe you are waiting for the person to spend the rest of your life with. But as life goes on, you will be in a waiting season for other things. In every phase of life you will have to go through this process. In every season you will be confronted with this question, "If you never get what you are praying for and believing for, *is He enough?*" This is so difficult and yet so necessary. Allowing the Lord to become enough *now* for you will release such peace and rest in you during the "waiting times" of life. If you grab hold of this revelation now, it will change everything.

Every one of us has asked for things we didn't get. We have believed for breakthroughs that didn't happen. We have fasted and prayed, and the miracle didn't come through. What do you do when things don't go as you hoped or prayed? How you respond to disappointment truly affects your destiny. I've seen people get angry, walk away from God, and become bitter, cynical people. They have no joy or peace. I've seen others lean into God even though they didn't understand the outcome. In those scenarios where people have leaned into Jesus, I have seen beauty arise out of the ashes. I want to be like the latter. Even when I don't understand, I still know my Jesus is good and kind. He loves me fully and completely and doesn't withhold any good thing from me. So, if something is being withheld, then maybe it's not good for me or maybe it's just not time. If I trust my Father, then I can trust His timing.

I know the question is scary and you may want to put the book down at this very moment. Don't allow the question to scare you off! The question has to be asked because this whole journey is about going deeper in the Lord. You and I have one life to live for Him. Let's live it to the fullest. I want your journey to be full of trust, full of peace, and full of joy. I don't know if you're going to get married, but I *do* know the Lord has some awesome things in store for you. If you trust Him, you will do things you never thought you would do, and He will use your life beyond what you ever imagined.

So, let me ask you again: Is He enough? If He is not, then be honest with Him. He is not afraid of your honesty. Tell Him what you're afraid of and why it's hard for you to trust Him with your dreams. Rather than push away from Him during this process, lean into Him. Allow Him to minister to your heart and heal the places that have allowed distorted truths to take root. He really is a good Father and if you don't know that, then allow Him to show you how good He really is.

ZERO IN ON:

➤ How you respond to disappointment truly affects your destiny.

➤ If you trust the Father, then you can trust His timing.

➤ Is God enough for you? This question and your response are a necessary part of the journey.

03

SURRENDERING TO HIS PROCESS

Giving things to the Lord is a process, and a difficult one at that. Every single time I was asked out on a date, I took it to the Lord to see if I had permission to go. Almost every single time I heard the Lord say, "No," and every single time I had to choose to surrender to the process.

If you don't know the love and kindness of the Lord, this can seem almost cruel, but it was anything but that. This wasn't the Lord being mean to me—this was the Lord keeping my heart in a place of trusting Him. He was protecting me, and I recognized that. There were times, especially in college and throughout my twenties, when I had to choose the boring Friday night at home because I was not going to hang out with a certain guy or be a part of the party scene. Settling was not an option. I had given the Lord all of who I was, and I wasn't going to allow a lonely night to draw me into a compromising relationship or situation. I'd rather be bored at home honoring God than out on a date with someone I knew the Lord had not given me permission to be out with. I turned down some very eligible men, which was not easy. At times, I missed going out because I knew that if I didn't have peace from the Lord, I couldn't go.

There were even seasons of my life where multiple guys pursued me at the same time, and then there were seasons where there was nothing and no one. Both were times of testing for my heart. When multiple guys pursued me, I took it before the Lord and heard Him say, "Not yet, daughter." I had to turn those guys down, trusting that if God wanted me to be in a relationship, then He would bring the right man. I believed that in that longed-for moment, not only would I have God's peace, I would also have His yes. In the times when there was no one pursuing me, I was tempted to take matters into my own hands and try to make it happen. But I knew this process was about staying in the posture of trusting God and allowing Him to lead me, not *me* lead me.

Both of those scenarios felt like the Lord was allowing me to choose once again. Would I continue to trust God and wait? Would I give up or allow Him to write my story? I repeatedly had to make the decision to stay in the posture of trust. By choosing to trust Him and wait on Him, I knew He would give me His best. I was confident that I could stand on that promise. *Choosing to trust God is waiting on His yes.* God's yes will lead you to places that will bless you beyond any of your expectations. He wants the best for you so you can trust both His no and His yes.

Walking it Out

Remember that prayer I prayed when I was nineteen? "Jesus, I give You my heart. Guard it, shield it, and give it back to me when You want me to give it away." Every time I went to the Lord and He told me no, He also said, "Not yet, daughter. See, I still have your heart. I'll give it back to you when I want you to give it away. I want you to trust Me in this journey."

Each time that happened, I had to reaffirm my commitment to the journey. I could choose to throw in the towel and just do what I wanted, or I could keep my posture of surrender and trust Him even when it was hard and uncomfortable. One of the greatest lessons I learned throughout this process was to stay in the journey the Lord had laid out for me and not jump ship when it got hard and I didn't understand. So many times we don't stay the course of the entire process. We tap out when it gets too hard and we get weary from choosing His way above our own. It's so hard to be patient when you don't know how long it will be or what the end result will look like. But when the issue of Lordship has been resolved in your life, you know you've given your life to Him, not in parts, but completely. My life was not my own anymore. My life was His and I trusted Him with all of it. The more I let go of control and let my dreams stay at His feet, the more I was confident that I was in the safest place I could be.

For nineteen years I had to walk this out. In response to every "No" from the Lord, I chose to praise Him and trust Him. Every year that passed, I chose to keep my feet planted in His promises over my life and not allow the enemy to distort this transforming process or the goodness and the faithfulness of God, which he tried to do many times. He tried to take advantage of the lonely nights and the moments when I felt the reality of my singleness. Each time, I had to allow the Lord to speak to my heart and remind me of His love for me and His promises over my life.

I also had to be intentional about not comparing myself to others. Even when I saw other people get what I desired, I had to choose to celebrate the reason for their joy and not withdraw and wallow in disappointment because I was still waiting. This perspective is so huge and necessary for the journey. One thing I was very intentional about during this process was celebrating other people's answered prayers. As I said earlier, I was a bridesmaid thirteen times and involved in over twenty weddings, so I got a lot of practice celebrating other people! Each time, I determined that I would be present and engaged in other people's moments. I often had to take time with the Lord and pour out my heart to Him before the event, allowing Him to bring me comfort and peace. I wanted my heart and head to be in the right space so that feelings of disappointment and pity wouldn't overtake me. Those celebratory moments weren't about me, they were about the people I loved. Because of that, I made sure they felt loved and celebrated by me. I recognized that it was both an honor and a joy to be part of their day and I was going to bring nothing but excitement and joy!

As the years passed, a belief system surfaced that I didn't even know I had. I began to think that if I did everything right, then I was somehow earning a blessing or answer to my prayers. It surfaced during a moment when I was spending time with the Lord. One of my friends was getting married, and I found myself, as usual, with no prospects and single as could be. As I sat there sharing my heart, I said, "Lord, when is this going to happen for me? When am I going to meet that person? I have followed You. I've done everything You've asked. I've laid this down for years. I've given You my heart. I've trusted You in this area. When is it my turn?"

As I heard my own words, I realized I had created conditions in my relationship with Jesus. If I was honest, there was a part of me that believed if I obeyed Him throughout this, He had to give me a husband because He *owed* it to me.

I remember the Lord saying, "Christa, you still don't truly trust Me. When I had you lay the dream of marriage on that altar, you didn't know if you were going to get it back. You still don't know, but know this, whether I have you get married or not, I still need the foundation of our relationship to be built on trust, and right now you don't fully trust Me. You are still trying to earn your blessings. I need you to trust Me despite how this turns out. I want you to get to a place where, if you never get married, you won't use it against Me. That can only happen when you know how much I love you and know how good I really am."

That conversation brought the final layer of surrender I needed. After that, I hit a place of total and complete contentment in being single. If I never got married, I wouldn't use it against God. I wasn't going to keep score of my good deeds and create a reward system in my relationship with the Lord anymore. I was going to trust Him, fully and completely. I was filled with joy and complete rest knowing the Lord truly had me covered. It wasn't something I could earn or control. I couldn't make it happen. I didn't want to make it happen. I wanted God to write my story, every part of it. So I stopped striving and started resting. For the first time, I was truly content, and that felt so good!

My Number One

To get to that place of true contentment and rest, we have to understand what the Lord is going after when He gives us the choice to surrender. When the Lord asked me if He was enough, I thought, *He's going after my number one.* God was going after my Isaac. I can recall the Lord saying, "I want to get you to a place, Christa, where you not only trust Me, you know that I'm good. The place where Jeremiah 29:11 is actually a revelation in your life, not just something you quote. I want you to actually believe that the plans I have for you are good. I want you to know that you can trust Me and that you know and believe I am a kind Father."

In the Bible, God asked Abraham the same type of question He asked me, but his scenario was much more extreme.

Abraham gave his life fully to God. He was a trusted disciple, a faithful follower. He and his wife were barren for years until, one day, the Lord prophesied a child over them. Being well past their baby-making years, they had a hard time believing the prophetic word, and took it into their own hands to make it happen. Sarah gave Abraham her maidservant to sleep with so she could produce the "promised child." If you are familiar with this story, then you know that Sarah's maidservant Hagar did, in fact, get pregnant and gave birth to Ishmael. But that pregnancy caused a whole other set of issues because this wasn't the way the Lord had designed His promise to take place. Where there had previously been peace between Sarah and Hagar, conflict arose. Isn't it amazing what gets disrupted when we put our hands on things that we aren't supposed to and create counterfeit versions of what God said He would do?

But the Lord, in His kindness, still opened Sarah's womb to conceive her own biological son. Eventually Sarah gave birth to Isaac, whose name means "laughter." I love that God named a child born to people barren and old "laughter." That is such a beautiful picture—God laughing at any obstacle. He wasn't worried or concerned about their old age. He planned on giving them a child—a son who would not only bring joy to their lives, but who would remind them daily of His faithfulness!

To understand the journey and process both Abraham and Sarah had to go through to see God's promise come to fruition, you have to know that decades passed where they were still barren. They had no child. No legacy. Think about how many baby dedications they went to, how many children's birthday parties they attended. Each occasion reminded them they would never be able to celebrate their own child's birthday's or dedication. I am sure they grieved heavily as their natural childbearing years came to an end. They thought it was over. The hope for a child would never be fulfilled. Then, God declared they would have a son! Wait, what? They thought that was off the table. They thought that would never be their story. Even with the word from God, they were nervous to hope, even scared to believe, but they let their hearts begin to entertain the possibility. The door opened again to a promise—a promise they never thought they would have. Then it didn't happen—at least not as quickly as they thought it would. So they waited and waited some more. Still it didn't happen. They began to wonder if maybe God didn't literally mean *their* child, but just a child with Abraham's seed. So Sarah convinced herself that maybe God didn't care if the promise included her, and decided her maidservant could serve as a surrogate for the promised child.

But God never wanted a surrogate. He wanted Abraham and Sarah to believe Him and trust Him. He wanted the promised child to come through the two of them. He wanted Abraham and Sarah to know He was not bound to age or biology! He wanted them to understand that if He prophesied it, then it would come to pass in His timing.

Years later, in Abraham's and Sarah's lives, we see the Lord go back to the same issue and address them in this area once again:

Some time later, God tested Abraham's faith.
"Abraham!" God called.

"Yes," he replied. "Here I am."

"Take your son, your only son—yes, Isaac, whom you love so much—and go to the land of Moriah. Go and sacrifice him as a burnt offering on one of the mountains, which I will show you."

The next morning Abraham got up early. He saddled his donkey and took two of his servants with him, along with his son, Isaac. Then he chopped wood for a fire for a burnt offering and set out for the place God had told him about. On the third day of their journey, Abraham looked up and saw the place in the distance.

"Stay here with the donkey," Abraham told the servants. "The boy and I will travel a little farther. We will worship there, and then we will come right back."

So Abraham placed the wood for the burnt offering on Isaac's shoulders, while he himself carried the fire and the knife. As the two of them walked on together, Isaac turned to Abraham and said, "Father?"

"Yes, my son?" Abraham replied.

"We have the fire and the wood," the boy said, "but where is the sheep for the burnt offering?"

"God will provide a sheep for the burnt offering, my son," Abraham answered. And they both walked on together. When they arrived at the place where God had told him to go, Abraham built an altar and arranged the wood on it. Then he tied his son, Isaac, and laid him on the altar on top of the wood. And Abraham picked up the knife to kill his son as a sacrifice.

At that moment the angel of the Lord called to him from heaven, "Abraham! Abraham!"

"Yes," Abraham replied. "Here I am!"

"Don't lay a hand on the boy!" the angel said. "Do not hurt him in any way, for now I know that you truly fear God. You have not withheld from me even your son, your only son."

Then Abraham looked up and saw a ram caught by its horns in a thicket. So he took the ram and sacrificed it as a burnt offering *in place of his son. Abraham named the place Yahweh-Yireh (which means "the Lord will provide"). To this day, people still use that name as a proverb: "On the mountain of the Lord it will be provided."* (Genesis 22:1-14 NLT)

Why did God ask this of Abraham? Because He wanted nothing to be withheld from Him. God was after a heart of complete surrender. In my life, even though I was a pastor in full-time ministry, God still went after the core of who I was. He went after my Isaac, and therefore, I questioned His character. I thought, *God if You're good, how in the world could You go after my one and only?*

But I heard God saying, "I *am* good. Even if I go after your one and only, that doesn't change Who I am. But you think it will. You think it does. So I actually want to address that. I want to break that false belief system in your life, because you've believed a lie about who I am."

To have a heart that doesn't hold anything back from the Father, you have to know how good He is. You have to know how much He loves you—how crazy in love with you He is. This is why He leads us into times in our lives where our faith is tested, just like Abraham's. In the area of singleness, my faith was tested on who I thought God was and His character. Questions surfaced like, "Am I really willing to trust Him with my deepest and most intimate desire? Can I really trust Him with my Isaac?" But when the Lord prophesies something over your life, there is nothing that is going to stop that word from coming to pass. It doesn't matter your age, your location, your abundance, or your lack. If the Lord wants to bless you, then He is going to bless you!

The Three-Day Journey

Have you ever noticed that sometimes when we wait and wait for a promise, when it finally comes to pass, we have to make sure that what we have waited for so long doesn't pull our affection away from the Lord? He wants us to enjoy our blessings and savor answered prayers, but He also wants to continue to be our "number one" above everything else. God won't share the first-place spot in our lives. He must be Lord over everything. When things begin to push the Lord out of His rightful place, He will lovingly bring that to our attention and ask us to put those things on the altar.

That is what was happening in the portion of Scripture we just read. Abraham was called to be a "father of many nations." With a destiny like that, the ultimate Father—Father God— invited Abraham on a three-day journey to lay his son, Isaac, on the altar of sacrifice. What kind of God asks for the promise He prophesied? What kind of Father asks for your only son? Because of Abraham's destiny to be a father to the nations, the Lord had to establish some foundational truths—that God was the supreme authority and the Lord of Abraham. He needed to see if He had all of Abraham's heart, even above his beloved Isaac, and if Abraham truly viewed Him as the Lord of his life.

Perhaps you are in the midst of your own three-day journey. The Lord is going after your heart in a deeper way and giving you the opportunity to choose Him above all else. He is going after your Isaac. Let's look deeper into what the Lord required of Abraham. By asking him to sacrifice Isaac, Abraham had to make certain preparations for this three-day journey.

1. He had to make sure his responsibilities were covered while he was out of town.

2. He had to arrange for some of his servants to accompany them on the trip.

3. He had to make sure they had all the supplies they needed.

4. Then he had to actually walk out the three-day journey.

There was nothing convenient or easy about this process. So many times, we think if it's that hard, then it can't be God. Many times, when it *is* that hard, it is from God. Let's remove our Western mentality of "I'm going to have it my way" in our relationships with the Lord. We live in a society that is all about convenience and making things as expedited and easy as possible. But we must understand that sometimes the places the Lord takes us are neither quick nor easy. Because of your destiny and what you carry, He is going after the foundation of your relationship with Him. He wants to heal every crack, restore every broken place, and overturn every injustice. Sometimes that takes time, and sometimes we have to do hard things to see the breakthrough in our lives.

What responsibilities is the Lord asking you to take care

of and cover in your season? Who do you need to ask to come with you on this journey? Are there trustworthy people who can keep you accountable in your decisions? What tools and resources do you have in place to keep you focused on the path before you? These preparations allow us to stay committed to our acts of surrender and submission.

Can you imagine being Abraham and having to walk beside your son, the promise and joy of your life, knowing the Lord has asked you to sacrifice him? Every step he took, it was as if he was saying, "I choose You, Lord. I choose You above everything. I'm all Yours, withholding nothing."

Think about your own life. This entire journey of singleness is your personal three-day hike to the altar of the Lord. He is not asking for your firstborn child in the natural, but He is asking for whatever has become the prerequisite for your joy, your happiness, your peace, or your obedience. Any condition or requirement you have created to be all in and completely surrendered to Jesus is your Isaac, and He is walking you to the altar. He is inviting you to lay it down, because He knows that if He isn't your number one, then you have a price, and if you have a price, that means you can be bought. The enemy will gladly pay any price to sideline you from your destiny.

If your price is money, then the enemy will do whatever he can to distract you with the desire and pursuit of money, distorting the truth that Jesus is your Source and your Provider. If your price is popularity and being an influencer on social media, then be sure that the enemy will get you so focused on being a cultural influencer you lose sight of being a kingdom influencer. If your price is being comfortable, then anytime the Lord asks something risky or hard, you'll believe the lie of the enemy that it couldn't possibly be God asking you to do hard things.

If you have a price, you will be bought. Through this three-day process, God saw that Abraham had no price, so he could never be bought. He was willing to sacrifice his only son, his child of promise, because Abraham only served one Master. You must understand that God is after your heart—your whole heart—and if you grab hold of this truth now, not only will your marriage be better for it, your life will also.

In verse 13, we read that the Lord provided the sacrifice for Abraham and he did not have to kill his son. It is oftentimes at the altar of sacrifice where the Lord will give you the answer you've been waiting for. It's in the final surrender that the breakthrough takes place. This takes time, just like a three-day journey in the wilderness takes time. Abraham's journey was dusty, dirty, and probably hot. If you have been uncomfortable in your journey, don't worry—it's not always going to be like that. At the same time, don't run from the dusty, dirty, or uncomfortable places. If the Lord is asking for what you hold dear, there is a reason. Trust Him more than you trust yourself.

My three-day journey was actually a three-year journey. Like Abraham, I had to make the choice to follow God—not just once, but every day of that journey. You and I have to choose every day whether we put God first. *Choice* is the foundation of this testing process. At any time, I could have made the choice to quit and give up, do things my own way. Daily, I chose to stay in the journey, and it was so worth it. Friends, you have to make your own choice to say yes. Choose to listen to Him. Choose to obey and choose to wait. The Lord gave us free will because He wanted us to choose Him and His ways above our own. He doesn't want puppets or forced lovers. He wants sons and daughters who want Him and choose Him above all else.

ZERO IN ON:

➤ Choosing to trust God is waiting on His yes.

➤ It is oftentimes at the altar of sacrifice where the Lord will give you the answer you've been waiting for.

➤ Be intentional about celebrating other people's answered prayers.

04

CONTENT YET CONTENDING

When the Lord asked me to lay down my dream of getting married, it was one of the most difficult things I had to do. Getting married was how I had always envisioned my life unfolding. Becoming a wife was the foundation on which I had built so many of my other dreams. Laying that dream down and trusting God with it was a deep and difficult journey for me. I knew He was asking me to lay marriage on the altar, but I didn't know if I would ever see the fulfillment of that dream or not. The act of laying down marriage meant I had to come to terms with the very real possibility that I may never get married at all.

To be in agreement with what the Lord was asking of me and truly lay this desire down, I had to fully let go of the dream. I had to face the reality that I may never know what it is to fall in love, loving someone completely and wholeheartedly. I may not get to have my dad walk me down the aisle, be intimate with a spouse, and build a family together. I may never experience what it meant to have someone so in love with me that they saw me as the woman of their dreams.

Letting go led me to the doorstep of grief. I didn't want to walk through that door, but I knew if I was truly going to arrive at a place of contentment, I would have to completely release the dream. The loss was layered and anything but simple. At every wedding and engagement announcement, I was faced with the looming reality of never experiencing any of those things. I had to grieve all of that to get to the place where I was at peace and resolved that if it never happened, I would be okay. I determined that I would fully trust the Lord with however my story turned out.

There is a certain tension all of us are going to experience. Throughout our lives, God is going to ask us to build Him altars of sacrifice on which to lay the things we have put before Him. He doesn't do this to punish us—not at all. He does this because He wants to be the One who receives our complete and total worship above anything else. He wants the hearts of His children to be fully given over to Him. Again, that was exactly what God was after with Abraham. Abraham was told to take the one he loved so much, the fulfillment of a promise and prophetic word, and lay it on the altar of sacrifice. The Lord wasn't doing this to be cruel. He did this to test Abraham's heart and see if He had all of it. Once God saw that Abraham's heart was fully committed to Him, He sent the angel of the Lord to tell Abraham not to harm his son. Instead, a ram caught in the thicket became the provision for the sacrifice. Abraham's heart was tested by the Lord and he passed it incredibly.

I believe that as Abraham made the trek to the altar of the Lord, he also believed God was going to provide the sacrifice. With every step Abraham made, it was as if he was saying, "I trust You God, and I will do what You ask of me. I will give You my son. But I also know You are good, and You can provide the sacrifice and spare my son, Isaac." God allowed Abraham to walk out this journey of consecration and surrender to reveal the posture of his heart.

Like Abraham, I was given my own test of the heart. I didn't know if I would ever get back what I put before the Lord, but I knew God never asks a question that doesn't have a purpose. The journey of singleness is also a journey to the altar of the Lord. Right now, you may be focused on the marriage altar, but God is focused on the altar of your heart. He wants to be your highest place of worship. That is what this journey is all about. It is about walking to the altar of the Lord to lay down marriage and trusting Him completely in the process. With every step you make to the altar of sacrifice, you are giving everything to the Lord, while simultaneously believing for the promises of God in your life.

Colliding with Grief

As I shared in the previous chapter, the stages of grief are not cut and dry. They can often overlap with one another, colliding and surfacing in the most unexpected moments. I remember in the midst of one extremely difficult day, the Lord reminded me of our "enough" conversation. He asked me again, "Christa, if you never get married, am I enough?"

I again responded, "You're not, but I need You to become enough." I continued to pray, "God, I want You to be enough, but honestly right now, You're not. But, if You want to become that in my life and You want me to go on that journey, then I say yes. I said yes to You at the age of three, and I said yes to this process of surrender at nineteen, and I am saying yes again at thirty-five. I have followed You my whole life. If this is what You're asking me to do, to lay marriage fully down, to completely trust You, then I will. If there's any belief within me that doesn't fully trust You for who You are, then take it out of me."

In the months and years that followed that moment, I often reflected back to it. It reminded me that even in a dark night of the soul, God comes through and brings fresh mercy and grace to keep you moving forward, even when you don't know how.

It was after that time that I began to process the grief. First came the anger. "God, how could You ask this of me? Of all things, why this?" Then came the bartering. "I'll give You this, God, if You just let me still get married. I'll give You anything else if You let me have that." Next, depression and disappointment that it may not take place rolled in. "God, is this actually not going to happen?" Then I felt angry all over again about the possibility that this may not happen for me.

I wish I could say this was a quick process, but it wasn't. This process lasted about eighteen months. I can't tell you the exact moment I entered into the "acceptance" phase, but I *can* tell you there came a day when God broke through once again and it felt finished. I had completely let it go and reconciled myself with the likely reality of never getting married. But regardless of the outcome, I trusted God completely. It took eighteen months of me laying that desire down again and again, choosing to stay in a posture of surrender and not hanging on to what He was asking me to let go of. If I could paint a picture of what this looked like for me, it would be of me kneeling before the Lord, worshiping Him with my hands wide open and extended before Him. That was truly the posture He led me to. In that process, Jesus truly became my Husband and my Refuge. He was my place of peace. When I stayed at His feet, it kept my eyes and my heart locked into why I laid my dream down in the first place—because it's all about Him.

Not too long after I entered the acceptance phase, I heard the Lord say to me, "Now, I'm going to teach you how to be *content* and yet *contend.*"

What Does It Mean to Be Content?

To be content is to be in a "state of satisfaction" and/or "to be satisfied."[2] I wanted to be a woman who was satisfied with where I was. I didn't want to live my days comparing my life to others, wishing I had what they had. I wanted to live from a place of gratitude for what I had been blessed with and not

2 s.v. "content," Dictionary.com.

be weighed down by what I didn't have or what I was still waiting for.

We all have areas in our lives where we wish we had made different decisions or that things had turned out differently. That is life. We can either choose to learn and move forward from these lessons, or allow them to hold us back in regret, disappointment, and remorse. Too many of us live from a place of disappointment rather than from a place of gratitude and contentment. I have found that being intentional and having gratitude in my life has unlocked a depth in my walk with the Lord. What I speak is an overflow of what I believe. Speaking life, hope, promise, joy, victory, and breakthrough is essential for gratitude to become my daily lifestyle. I am not talking simply about positive confessions—I am talking about declaring the promises of God over your life!

We see this in the life of David through the Book of Psalms. What I love about David is that he is honest and vulnerable before the Lord. He doesn't hide how he is feeling from God, but always comes back to a place of worship and exaltation of *who* God is, even in the toughest of trials. This is so key. If you want to stay in a place of contentment, you cannot let your emotions and feelings overtake you. I know it's very trendy to be "all up in your feelings," but our feelings change from day to day, and for some, from hour to hour. You cannot base your life around things that are so fluid and inconsistent. I may have a feeling or emotion about a person or situation, but if it's not rooted in the Word and Jesus, I am not coming into agreement with it.

Negative emotions are a part of our humanity. We have them, but what we do with them is up to us. If I am feeling frustrated during the day, I need to stop and ask myself, "What is really going on? Am I frustrated about a specific situation or is it something deeper? Is there a conversation I need to have? When is the last time I spent time in the presence of God?" When I take time to assess the negative emotions, I keep them from provoking my conversations and actions. I don't allow them to drive me, mold me, or define me.

Remember, David was mocked and persecuted, faced multiple death threats, and made some horrible decisions. Yet, he always came back to prayer, worship, and praise. David is referred to as a "man after God's own heart." He was not called that because he always got it right, but because no matter what, he always turned to God. He was a worshiper, an exalter of God's Word. Like David, we are not always going to get it right and we are not always going to make the perfect decision. We will come up short, mess up, or act impulsively. Yet in all things, let us be led back to the Lord and His heart for us. To be a person of contentment is to be one who worships and exalts God. It is a posture of worship and gratitude, exalting and praising God, that keeps everything in perspective and keeps our hearts rooted in truth, not just in our feelings.

When I declare the promises of God over my life, it brings things into focus. It makes me aware of how the Lord has blessed me! Declaring the promises of God and His Word over me has become a lifeline of hope in times of pain and disappointment. Many times I have cried out to God through tears, declaring His truth and His promises over me, even when it is in direct contradiction to what I am facing in the natural.

Being a person who is content is being a person who is *grateful*—grateful for what the Lord has done in my life and grateful for what He is still doing in my life!

I remember a moment when a friend of mine was getting married to a guy I had once been interested in. I knew they were supposed to be together and their union was definitely a God match. But when their engagement was announced, I remember the enemy immediately knocked on my door, throwing every lie of rejection and disappointment my way. Of course I was disappointed. But I chose to sow *joy* into a very difficult moment. I chose to not let my feelings overtake me or allow the lies of the enemy to become my truth. That didn't mean denying how I felt. I am very in touch with my feelings and emotions. However, I also recognize not everything I feel is from the Lord, and I chose to make His truth higher than what I felt.

Every one of us can look around at other people's lives and see things we would love to have. But we stay content when we focus on the blessings we already have. For some people, it may be harder to find the beauty in your surroundings when all you see is ashes. But if you start digging, I promise you will find gold. Those blessings may be good health, a strong mind, a job that's fulfilling, people who love you, a roof over your head, food in your refrigerator, a car to drive, or money in your bank account. And what about blessings in the Spirit? You are saved, love Jesus, and He loves you. He has plans for you, a future that is bright and full of promise. You walk in freedom because of Jesus. Shame and addiction have been broken off your life. You are no longer depressed or suicidal because Jesus set you free! Take the time even now to thank God for *everything* He has blessed you with! Seeing the beauty in your life is such a key part in being content.

Another key to being content is removing the need for instant gratification. In the society we live in, if there is not an immediate benefit or gratification, many times we either do not value something or stick with something until the end. Looking for instant gratification keeps you shortsighted and robs you of the blessing of completing the entire process of your journey. When people are driven by instant gratification, they have a hard time seeing beyond the moment, which isn't a wise place to live from. Not only will it leave you discontent, but there are numerous valuable things in life that don't give you immediate results or the immediate breakthrough you were hoping for. The benefits of those choices, habits, or life-styles will only be seen over time. When you are shortsighted, you miss out on the long-term benefits waiting for you.

I've always had this type of relationship with exercise. I work out a lot, but my body may not always look like it. That's because my weight is more determined by diet than exercise. I have to adjust my diet if I want my weight to shift, but exercise keeps me toned, healthy, and fit overall. Both are important to me, but if I were only after a number on a scale I would just be focused on diet. Instead, overall health is my priority, so I lift weights, train in Krav Maga, and do cardio workouts. I don't always see the immediate results I want, but I know, over time, I will reap the benefits of working out.

Recently, I went to the doctor for a physical and all my numbers came back really good. All of the tests checked off components you and I don't see, but are vital to our health. I work out mainly for the things I don't see, which means I have to shift my mindset for what my motive is. It is irrelevant whether people look at me and wonder if I work out or not. I know I do, and I know my health is better for it. I am going after something greater than what I look like—success in my overall health. That takes time. It's not always fun. I don't always feel like it, but I keep doing it because the long-term benefit is worth it. If I was only driven by instant gratification, I wouldn't work out that much, but in the long run, my health would be seriously affected by lack of exercise.

Our spiritual life is a lot like this. We can see someone preach and move in the gifts and be in awe of how incredible a communicator and minister they are. But that's just the outward expression. As a follower of Jesus, I want my inner walk with Him to be the strongest part of our relationship. I don't want to be the preacher who can hype a crowd and fill an auditorium because of what I bring. I want people to be drawn to *Jesus in me*. I want Him to be what people experience when I minister, not just another polished preacher.

But I have a confession. I don't always want to read the Word, pray, worship, or spend time with the Lord. Not because I don't love Him. I love Him so much. But sometimes I get distracted and allow the busyness of life to pull me away from time with Him. As I've matured, I've realized that regardless of whether I feel like it or not, I must spend time with the Lord. It is literally essential to my spiritual health. When I spend time in the presence of God, it settles my soul (mind, will, and emotions). Spending time in God's presence allows His peace to overtake me, and anxiety cannot stay. When I pray and empty my heart before the Lord, there is a divine exchange that takes place where He takes my burdens and fills me with His peace. I may not feel something every day, but I know, in time, there are immeasurable benefits to reading His Word, praying, and spending time in His presence.

Another key to being content is found in Psalm 37:4 (NIV):

> *Take delight in the Lord, and He will give*
> *you the desires of your heart.*

As we delight ourselves in the Lord, rather than being focused on being gratified, we will find ourselves in a greater place of peace and joy. Another way to say it is, it's better to be focused on delighting myself in the Lord, because the more we delight ourselves in Him, the less frustrated and unfilled our lives will be. The joy and fulfillment in our lives will only be found in Him. He is our greatest joy and gift, but we can only experience this when we spend time with Him.

I've had lots of conversations with people about their walk with the Lord, and when the topic of "contentment" comes up, many people find it difficult to fathom a life where they are truly at peace and satisfied. But I believe Scripture is clear that this life is not only available to us—it is part of our inheritance as children of God. You and I can live satisfied and content with who we are in Christ Jesus and what He has given us. Everything we *need*, He will supply:

> *And my God will meet all your needs according to the riches of his glory in Christ Jesus.*
> (Philippians 4:19 NIV)

You and I may have a lot of *wants*, and we may not have all of them at this present moment, but He will always supply what we *need*. Needs and wants are two different things. As much as I have wanted things in my life, I have to recognize that just because I want it doesn't mean I need it. To take it one step further, if I don't have it and the Father hasn't supplied it, then I don't need it for this season of my life. That doesn't mean He won't give it to me in the future, but I can rest and be content in the fact that whatever I need, He will provide it in His timing.

To be content ultimately comes down to trust. If you don't believe that God has your best interest in mind, then you won't truly trust Him. And if you don't truly trust Him, then you will never be content. If you find yourself discontent, often comparing your life to other people's lives and dissatisfied with where you are, then really it comes back to the issue of trusting God.

One can argue that sometimes we are dissatisfied because we have settled, and we were created for more. I wouldn't disagree with that. Being discontented can often push us to press in for the more. I've seen that in my own life. I have had places where I have been dissatisfied and the dissatisfaction provoked a change within. But right now, I am talking about a core level in your personal theology. Do you fully trust God, believing He has your best interest in mind? Do you believe He is truly the supplier of your needs and your source? If you don't trust Him, your beliefs will not be anchored. You will not be content, and your heart will not be at rest.

Here is what Paul says in Philippians 4:11-13 (NIV):

> *I am not saying this because I am in need, for I have learned to be content whatever the circumstances. I know what it is to be in need, and I know what it is to have plenty. I have learned the secret of being content in any and every situation, whether well fed or hungry, whether living in plenty or in want. I can do all this through Him who gives me strength.*

We all know the famous verse, "I can do all this through Him who gives me strength." It's true. You can do all things through Him because He is your source of strength. But look at the beginning of that verse. Paul had learned to be content in all things. He was content whether he had little or a lot. He was content in every situation. How? Because He understood that God was his source and would give him what he needed— not necessarily what he may have wanted.

Does the Lord care about our wants and desires? Absolutely. But we cannot make our wants and desires a requirement for our love, affection, or trust in Him. Paul understood this truth. Paul gave his life totally and completely to Jesus. This was a man who one day was persecuting and murdering Christians, and after one encounter with God, was radically transformed, becoming one of the greatest proclaimers of the gospel. He was all in. There was nothing in his life that hadn't been surrendered to the Lord. He was not living for himself—he was living for Jesus Christ.

There is so much we can learn through the life of Paul. He was surrendered, completely reliant and fully committed to the cause of Jesus. Everything about his life was surrendered to the King. Friends, that same surrender, that same "all in" lifestyle we see with Paul, is what you and I are called to. When we give our lives to the Lord, we are saying He is now Lord of our lives, not us. Under His Lordship, we can trust that He will give amazing blessings and gifts to us, but it may not always be in the timeline or package we are expecting. Paul learned to be content, which is another way of saying that he trusted God completely. Let's follow the example of Paul and lay at our Savior's feet the desires of our hearts, knowing we can be content in trusting Him.

Lastly, let's avoid the comparison trap. That trap is set by the enemy to compare the blooper reels of our lives to the highlight reels of other people. People often show us the best, edited, and prettiest versions of themselves and their lives. They don't show you the dirty bedroom and bathroom where they are taking that perfect selfie. They cut, edit, and filter every picture so what is posted is merely a very manipulated version of what is real. But many of us get sucked into believing this facade is real and it's the whole picture. Nothing could be further from the truth. Every person has their battles, struggles, and challenges. I once heard my husband say that if everyone threw their problems into the middle of a circle, each of us would be pulling our own back out because we wouldn't trade them for anyone else's. Seeing what others are going through puts things into perspective. Maybe what you're dealing with isn't as bad as you thought.

When we fall into the comparison trap, we are no longer able to celebrate other people's blessings and breakthroughs. It's difficult to be happy for someone when you feel bad because you didn't get their blessing. If I have learned anything about being content, it has been to be content with what the Lord is doing in my life and to celebrate other people in their break-throughs. When you live in that place, the fulfilled dreams of others begin to testify to you, reminding you that if God did it for them, then He can certainly do it for you! If you are caught in the comparison trap, then you will miss the blessing of the testimony!

Remember how I shared in Chapter 1 that I was involved in over twenty weddings? Well, that was practice in learning the lesson of contentment. As I said before, at most of those events, I had to take some time with the Lord to make sure I was walking in peace. I wanted to be fully able to celebrate and participate in my amazing friends' special days! I refused to make it about me. Being in a place of contentment is when you are able to celebrate someone else having what you want. You can't celebrate what you are envying, and you can't be present when you are discontent. You won't wait on the Lord to write your story if you are looking for instant gratification. Contentment, my friend, is trusting God and knowing that He is supplying everything you need in *this* season of your life. You can trust that He is who He says He is—a good Father.

What Does It Mean to Contend?

Every one of us knows what it is like to contend for something the Lord has spoken over you to become reality. Contending is when you are believing for a promise to come to pass or a breakthrough you've been praying for to happen.

Contending is connected to your level of faith. If you don't think something is going to happen, then your heart won't engage with it, nor will you fight for it to happen. Our faith is an essential part of our contending. We read in Hebrews 11:1, *"Now faith is confidence in what we hope for and assurance about what we do not see"* (NIV). Contending is standing on the faith of what we hope for and the assurance about what we believe God is going to do. Contending isn't passive or apathetic. Contending is where agreement and confidence meet and release faith to believe that if God said it, then it will come to pass. Contending is about believing, regardless of what you see in the natural. This isn't to endorse or promote delusional or fantasy thinking, but it is to enforce the truth that we are called to be people of faith. Often, what we are believing in the natural doesn't seem likely. But because we serve a God whose signature move is doing the impossible, faith slides right in, empowering us to believe His Word above anything else.

When I looked up synonyms for contend, I found the words *battle, fight,* and *maintain.* Contending requires a fight within us to rise up and oppose what comes against that promise. How do I battle against opposition? With His Word. I write down Scriptures and create declarations of what the Lord says. I keep notes in my phone of daily declarations that I pray out, believing that my words of declaration win the battle and *maintain* my position of faith. This allows me to remain in agreement with what the Lord has said.

Maintaining a position of faith is not always easy. But as I speak His promises over me and pray into the prophetic words I have received, or the things He has whispered to me as I have spent time with Him, I create a memorial of what God has said. That is what I set my heart on. That is what I base my contending on. At times, I grew weary in contending and believing, yet I pressed on. I continued to come back to what the Lord had said. Even when years kept passing by, I kept standing on His promise and truth that if I was supposed to get married, God would bring me that person. He would do it, not me. It required me to trust His ways and His timing above my ways and my desired timing.

One thing I have learned through the years is the importance of not entertaining contrary thoughts to what I am contending for. I call this the "What if" train. This train never takes me to a good place. If I jump on it, I find myself going down tracks of worst-case scenarios and failed end results. It's never uplifting, and it certainly doesn't help me maintain my position of contending and believing.

Sometimes, protecting my posture also means doing some really practical safeguards. When I was contending for my husband and the promises of God, but wanting to guard the delicate tension of being content with my life, there were certain romantic movies I couldn't watch. There were books I didn't read and music I couldn't listen to. If I did, I found myself with cravings, leaving my place of peace because emotions and desires got stirred up. I learned that, although the movies and entertainment were clean—it was never a moral issue, it was simply watching people fall in love—I needed to protect the position of my heart. These beautiful love stories didn't guard my peace. If something undermines your peace and you find yourself anxious after talking to a friend or watching a certain movie, reconsider allowing that into your life during your times of waiting. There were other times in my nineteen-year journey that I felt relatively unaffected by love stories and could watch them with no problem. Pay attention to guarding your peace and your process. Recognize that when you entertain things that disrupt your place of faith, they need to be removed. No movie, conversation, book, song, or whatever is worth robbing you of your peace and contentment.

Here are some questions to ask yourself as you contend:

1. What has the Lord spoken to me concerning my singleness?

2. What Scripture has He given me to contend with?
3. What are the promises of God over my life?
4. Who does He say I am?

Answering these questions will position you in a place of being rooted in what God is saying so that when the "What if" train pulls up, you will not be tempted to get on. It's not always easy, but in Christ you have everything you need to remain in this place.

A Beautiful Tension

Content yet contending for the promises of God—this is what I call a beautiful tension. It's gratitude for who you are in Christ Jesus and what you have in your life, while still believing for more. Being content and satisfied doesn't mean you can't believe or desire for more. It simply means that you are agreeing and contending for the "more" of God in a specific area and also resting in the place of contentment, knowing He is your source, while trusting Him completely. It's a delicate tension and place you have to intentionally abide in.

Again, when the Lord asked me the question, "Christa, if you never get married, am I enough?" I told Him, "You're not, but I want You to be." The process of going from Him not being enough to Him becoming enough was the process of me learning how to be content with what I did have in my life and accepting that if my life never changed, I was sincerely happy and fulfilled. It didn't remove the desire for marriage, but it did remove it as a requirement for happiness. It is so imperative that you catch this. Before the process of laying down marriage, marriage was a *requirement* for me to be happy. After I laid it down, it became a *desire* to be married. It was no longer a requirement for my happiness nor was it a requirement for my destiny. This tension of being content yet contending can only co-exist when our requirements and desires are surrendered to Jesus. When you surrender these to Jesus, you can trust Him with His plans and purposes. He does give us the desires of our heart, but our desires are sanctified when they have first been surrendered.

I think this is such an important place for all of us to live. In your singleness, I believe this place of trusting, yet believing for more, is the place where the greatest level of peace can be tapped into. It is the place where you stay connected to what God is doing in the present moment. It removes an unhealthy focus on the future. It keeps your heart connected with who God is right now in your life and keeps you agreeing with what He is going to do. It roots you in peace and removes any access points for anxiety to creep in.

You know you are in this beautiful tension when there is a peace within you that, no matter what happens, you are going to be okay because you know God has you. You can trust Him with your dreams and desires, and you aren't afraid anymore of things not turning out as you thought they would. Instead, you trust, believe, and abide in the truth that, regardless of the end result, you have an incredible destiny you are called to walk out. You are fully confident that God has awesome things in store for you! You let go of all of your previous requirements to be happy or fulfilled, and you start pursuing the call of God on your life. You start living your life and who you were called to be fully and completely.

You know you are living in this beautiful tension when friends get engaged and you are sincerely happy. When you receive the fulfillment of their dream as a testimony that if God can do it for them, He can do it for you! Other people's breakthroughs are no longer painful reminders of what you don't have. Instead, they are opportunities to celebrate and enjoy the community the Lord has blessed you with.

It was a process for me to get to this point. I had to lay things down. I had to grieve the reality that there were some desires in my life that may not come to pass. But when I walked through the entire process, not staying in the grief, continuing to move forward, leaning into Him even when it was hard, I found myself trusting at a core level and believing in the goodness of God. Therefore, whatever happened, I knew I would be okay and live a fulfilled life because He had finally become enough for me.

ZERO IN ON:

➤ **When I declare the promises of God over my life, it brings things into focus.**

➤ **Contentment is trusting God and knowing that He is supplying everything you need in this season of your life.**

➤ Contending is where agreement and confidence meet and release faith to believe that if God said it, then it will come to pass.

➤ He does give us the desires of our heart, but our desires are sanctified when they have first been surrendered.

05

HOW COME I'M THE ONLY ONE?

Social media can be a great tool to connect, but it can also be the archnemesis to you keeping your peace in being single. Think about what I shared on comparison in the last chapter. When you are struggling with your singleness, it's amazing how it can feel like everyone on social media is posting about their new boo, engagement, and wedding. As you look through different posts, what started off as a quick social media scroll on a Saturday afternoon ends up completely bumming you out. Now all you want to do is binge Netflix and eat a pint of Ben & Jerry's. Okay, so maybe I've been tempted a time or two to go there!

Seriously, the triggers social media can produce are real, and you need to know how to recognize your limits. There are days when I may be battling with something, fighting for my peace or joy, and I know going on social media may not be the wisest activity for me that day. So, I choose to not go on social media to guard my peace. It's not weak to say that something can trigger you. Nor is it weak to recognize you don't have the capacity for a certain situation or conversation that day. Sometimes as Christians, we think we are invincible. We aren't, but Jesus is. And yes, He dwells within us and we have access to overcome all things through Him, but there are times we are vulnerable and need to be careful of what we expose ourselves to. To me, that is just using wisdom.

I recently learned a term called "norm matching."[3] It's typically used when talking to people about their eating habits. Research shows there is a natural pressure in social settings to match those around you and do what others are doing—hence the term "norm matching." Social behaviorists have studied that people will naturally behave like the people around them they consider "normal." We naturally want to "match" those around us, and because of that core desire of wanting to be accepted, we often will mimic what we see around us.

Although the term "norm matching" typically applies to eating, I think it is a great term to apply across the board. Society tells us when we should accomplish certain key events in our lives—going to college, moving out of the house, owning our own home, deciding what career we are going to have, getting married, having children, and the list goes on. When

3 Suzanne Higgs & Jason Thomas. "Social Influences on Eating." *Science Direct*, October 5, 2015. https://www.sciencedirect.com/science/article/pii/S235215461500131X)

our core desire is to be loved and accepted, and we find our-selves out of sync with that timeline, we can easily feel left out and behind. But what if I offered you the idea that you are not behind, but right on time with *God's* timeline for your life?

"For I know the plans I have for you,"
declares the Lord, "plans to prosper you and
not to harm you, plans to give you hope and
a future." (Jeremiah 29:11 NIV)

The Lord created you with a destiny and a purpose! He knows the timing of your life. Society has created these time-lines we are expected to follow, but they don't necessarily line up with heaven's timing for you. I truly believe you and I are called to follow the order of heaven throughout our lifetime. That includes when we get married, have children, etc. When we break out of the social pressure box and give ourselves permission to be different, being who God has called us to be *unapologetically*, it releases such freedom for us and also for other people.

That level of freedom is God's intention for our lives, for us to not blindly fit in to what others are doing around us. Consider what Paul says in the Book of Romans:

Do not conform to the pattern of this world
but be transformed by the renewing of your
mind. Then you will be able to test and

*approve what God's will is—his good, pleas-
ing and perfect will.* (Romans 12:2 NIV)

If we are not careful, we can fall into the trap of "norm matching" and put unnecessary pressure on ourselves when we see people around us dating, getting engaged, and getting married. I love how The Message translation drives home this verse even further:

> *So here's what I want you to do, God help-
> ing you: Take your everyday, ordinary life—
> your sleeping, eating, going-to-work, and
> walking-around life—and place it before
> God as an offering. Embracing what God
> does for you is the best thing you can do for
> him.* **Don't become so well-adjusted
> to your culture that you fit into it
> without even thinking. Instead, fix
> your attention on God.** *You'll be changed
> from the inside out. Readily recognize what
> he wants from you, and quickly respond to
> it. Unlike the culture around you, always
> dragging you down to its level of immaturity,
> God brings the best out of you, develops well-
> formed maturity in you.* (Romans 12:1-2
> MSG, emphasis added)

Comparing your journey to someone else's journey is not only unproductive—it can put so much unnecessary pressure on you. It is God who knows and has the best specifically for you. Not only that, what He has for you is intended to bring out the best in you, changing you from the inside out as you walk out your unique process.

Every person has a unique journey. I certainly saw it in my own family. As I shared earlier, I am the youngest of three girls and my sisters and I have very different stories from one another. My middle sister got married at twenty-two years old, and they just celebrated their twenty-fifth wedding anniversary. My oldest sister didn't get married till she was thirty-one years old, and I didn't get married till I was thirty-nine years old. So, what's my point? My point is that all of us married exactly who I believe the Lord had for us, but all our journeys looked very different from one another. If I had based my peace and trust in God on my middle sister's story, I would have only had a precedent for peace until age twenty-two, and for the next seventeen years, I would have been riddled with striving and anxiety. The same would have been true if I had compared myself to my oldest sister's story. I would have trusted God and had peace until I was thirty-one years old, but as soon as that birthday passed, I would have been disappointed. It would be eight years until I was married myself. By taking on someone else's timeline as your story, you set yourself up for unmet expectations and a lot of frustration.

For nineteen years, when I asked the Lord if I could date certain guys, all I heard was "No." So, I waited. In nineteen years, I think I went on four dates total, and in each of those situations I did not have the peace of the Lord to move forward into anything more. So, I chose to allow the peace of the Lord to be my guide and assurance of His leading and blessing. If I did not have His peace, I did not move forward. Period. Even if you hear "No" for nineteen years straight, I believe it's better to be single and happy than married and miserable. God's peace is your guide. Never stray from it.

What can be a real challenge as you wait is not getting sucked into "norm matching." I saw those around me dating people and doing things I knew I didn't have permission to do. There were moments I found myself weary of being the only person not in a relationship or being the constant third wheel when hanging out. But I recognized that if the Lord put His plans and His destiny within me, He knew the perfect timing, and I had to trust that.

In your life, you will have people with whom you are in close relationship who will make very different decisions than you. Just because they are making those decisions, and even at times compromising core values, you shouldn't allow their standards and convictions to become your own. Remember Romans 12:1-2. Not only do we not need to submit to the timeline of those around us, but we also can't allow their decisions to drag us down to immaturity in our faith.

Even when those around me were making very different decisions than I was, I knew I had to stay true to the convictions the Lord put within me. What other people could do had nothing to do with what I knew I was allowed to do and not do. I had to make a choice not to submit to others' standards. In a world where peer pressure is real, you must know who you are called to be and the convictions He has instilled within you. Even in the church, there are people who will make very different decisions than you. But understand, when Jesus is Lord of your life, His convictions must become your convictions. His standards must become your standards.

When you are post-thirty-five and single, you hit the realization that your story may not look like everyone else's story. I was knee-deep in celebrating everyone's milestone moments, and when I looked at my life, it was so different than those around me.

At thirty-five, I found myself overworked, exhausted, and moving back home with Mom and Dad to regroup from the intensity of the previous season. I had lost the condo I had purchased due to the failing economy and a real estate market that had bottomed out. My condo was worth only a third of what I had purchased it for. Then, during the move back home, my car was stolen. I went to take a friend to the airport and my car was gone. Eleven days later, it showed up on the side of the freeway stripped down to its outer shell. I had just put a significant amount of money into replacing its engine and fixing other things. Since I owned it outright, I wanted to avoid a car payment during my time of transition, but that plan didn't go as I expected. So there I was at thirty-five, with no home and a stolen car, moving back in with Mom and Dad, and with my health needing some repair due to prolonged stress. Three years later, I had become the associate pastor at a church and gotten another car, but I was still living with Mom and Dad, and all my personal belongings were still in storage. I was single in every sense of the word, and I didn't see any viable options for marriage around me.

I share this simply to illustrate that sometimes in life, we find ourselves in situations and circumstances we did not expect to be in. How I respond in these moments, especially in ones I don't like, is critical to whether I'm going to grow while going through them. When I get frustrated and complain about challenging circumstances, I don't grow. Instead, I regress, allowing the irritation of the situation to eat away at my peace and my joy, ultimately robbing me of the opportunity to learn and mature. It is when I embrace and lean into the hard things that I have seen the Lord expand my perspective. He increases compassion and empathy within me so that when I encounter others who may have walked a similar path, I am able to bring a testimony of hope and breakthrough. I will miss out on that testimony and the opportunity to use the hard things to help others if I'm constantly focusing on what I don't like about my life or the challenges I am facing. My husband once said, "Ninety percent of warfare is perspective." I couldn't agree more. All of us will find ourselves in situations and circumstances we didn't see coming. But God is never surprised, and He is always in control, working everything together for His glory. Trusting Him and focusing on Him are what will keep you grounded and at peace in the turmoil that tries to overtake you through the unexpected twists and turns of life.

It is in those moments you really have to understand that maybe your timeline looks different because God is doing something different with you. I had to let go of people's expectations and the pressures of society, and settle into a place of wanting God's timing for my life above my own desires. Man, is that hard. It's so hard.

One of the key things I did in my life was surround myself with people who didn't shame me for my singleness. They didn't make me feel bad or less than for not being married. In the church world, this shame is real. Although it's often with good intentions, people will remind you of your age, biological clock, lack of options, and the list goes on. Engaging in those conversations isn't life-giving or helpful to a person who is trying to guard their peace. It's okay to put up boundaries with people who try to go there with you. Eventually, I realized that many of the people who wanted access to the private places of my heart were not in close relationship to me. Nope, sorry. I don't give access to the tender places of my heart to acquaintances. Those places are reserved for close family and friends I know and trust, people I have a track record with and who I know will speak from a place of encouragement. I would encourage you to use wisdom in sharing your heart, and especially who you allow to speak to those tender areas of your heart. People I barely knew wanted to know all about my nonexistent love life and how I felt being thirty-seven and single. Those are conversations for your inner circle, not the random person who just wants to be in the know. It's okay to set boundaries. It's not rude or mean. It's actually very healthy, and I learned, over time, to do that in order to guard my peace.

I do think, the majority of the time, people have good motives. They care and want what is best for you. But what people often lack is self-awareness about when they are projecting their fears and issues on you. I don't know how many times people asked me how I could do what I did as a pastor in my later thirties while being single. They went on to share how, if it were them, they would be at home depressed and eating a gallon of ice cream, but they were happy I was doing so well with my "situation." Someone telling me they would be depressed if they had my life was not the encouragement I was looking for. Thank the Lord He gave me thick skin (most of the time), because I was able to laugh it off and move on. But I think there are a lot of people who find it incredibly hard to be single. When people project their own fears onto others, it is not only unhelpful, it can also serve as a trigger and disrupt the peace of those walking out that process. We need to be mindful of what comes out of our mouths and what we speak over others as well as ourselves. People's opinions about your journey of singleness are irrelevant, so creating healthy boundaries is a good thing as you walk this out.

Here is the bottom line. Not everyone is going to be comfortable with you being single and being at peace about it. I was thirty-eight years old, single, and happy, but some people were concerned that I wasn't out doing everything I could do to meet a man. Your contentment may bother someone else, but recognize that it is not your responsibility to make them comfortable with your journey. Your only responsibility is to trust the Lord and live in peace. When we live in peace, it slaps the lies of the enemy in the face and breaks any influence of the wrong narrative. Don't let anyone disrupt that or pull you from a place of trusting in God. Your story is about you and Jesus. Walk it out with confidence.

Trusted with a Unique Call

When you have this perspective, the question shifts from *"Why am I the only one?"* to *"Why have I been trusted with this journey?"* Abraham could have easily wondered why he was being singled out. Why was God asking for his son and not someone else's? It's simple—because of Abraham's destiny. Abraham wasn't called to live an ordinary life without impact. He was called to be a father of the faith, the great patriarch! Abraham and his offspring were destined to transform and bring redemption to the earth. What a destiny! Because of the call on Abraham's life, God asked him to make some choices that would position him most effectively for his destiny.

Like Abraham, your place in history is undeniable. The blueprint of how God is going to use you wasn't ever meant to be a copy—it was always meant to be an original. You are singled out because God wants you to carry His distinction. The purpose and original intent over your life wasn't to duplicate someone else's. Your genetic coding is unique. Your eye retina and fingerprints are all one-of-a-kind for a reason. It is the power of uniqueness. It is the power of one life created by God to be fully original. Our God is not a cookie-cutter God. He has always used the uniqueness of who He created us to be. We all want to be used for God's *purposes*; therefore, we must first be God's *person*. In order to be God's person, you have to go through God's *process*. He isn't like McDonald's, where no matter which McDonald's you eat at, it's always the same. God has never worked that way. He created all of us to be different and unique, all with His plans and purposes in mind.

This knowledge should stir up excitement in you, because the more unique your journey, the more unique your destination! When it comes to your destiny and the part you play in the greater purposes of God, God is not interested in using a doppelganger. He wants to use you! Your uniqueness is one of your greatest traits. God has to do something distinct in you to pull something distinct out of you. He has placed you in this world to make the impact only you can make. So why would this not apply in the area of relationships? The decisions you make as you walk out the call on your life are vital, and the person you invite into your life, with intimate access to your heart, matters. He has trusted you with whatever process you are in to form you into everything He wants you to be. He singles you out because His gaze is firmly fixed on you, watching your every move, delighting in your growth, and anticipating the revealing of all the good things He has prepared just for you.

ZERO IN ON:

➤ How you respond each moment, especially when you don't like it, is critical to whether you are going to grow while going through it.

➤ Maybe your timeline looks different because God is doing something different with you.

➤ Your uniqueness is one of your greatest traits. God has to do something distinct in you to pull something distinct out of you.

➤ The decisions you make as you walk out the call of God on your life are vital, and the person you invite into your life, with intimate access to your heart, matters.

06

THE "D" WORD

It wasn't till I was thirty-five years old that I got to the place where I was really ready to get married. Up until that point, it was definitely a desire, but it wasn't a driving force in my life. Then thirty-five came, and all the grace that I had previously walked in was suddenly nowhere to be found.

Desperation is one of those funny things. It will bring things out in you that you never knew were there. The behavior and decisions you have possibly passed judgement on others for, you will find yourself now considering. Desperation is one of those emotions that can overwhelm and easily take over if you're not careful. It can feel like an ocean swallowing you up. The peace you were walking in yesterday feels unattainable the next day. When the grace lifted for me at thirty-five, I found myself no longer enjoying my singleness, and patience in waiting was nonexistent.

You may be in your twenties feeling this way. That is okay. Regardless of the age at which you find feelings of desperation creeping in, I want to encourage you to remember that you are not alone. Right now, I want you to take a deep breath. Breathe in the peace of the Lord and exhale all stress, worry, and anxiety. Do this a few times and let His help settle your heart and emotions. As you repeat this process, meditate on His truth that you are not alone. Keep repeating the statement, "I am not alone. Jesus has me." I do this myself when I am facing a situation in which I know I've lost perspective. If I feel desperate, it usually means I believe the outcome solely relies on me, when the truth is, it relies on Jesus. I have nothing to fear or worry about. The truth is that the Lord has me, He has you, and He is taking care of everything.

But desperation is real and it's not always negative. Desperation can produce a beautiful, passionate pursuit in you for the promise and breakthrough you've been praying for. We see this in the Bible through the life of Hannah:

> *Hannah was in deep anguish, crying bitterly as she prayed to the Lord. And she made this vow: "O Lord of Heaven's Armies, if you will look upon my sorrow and answer my prayer and give me a son, then I will give him back to you. He will be yours for his entire lifetime, and as a sign that he has been dedicated to the Lord, his hair will never be cut." As she was praying to the Lord, Eli watched her. Seeing her lips moving but hearing no sound, he thought she had been drinking. "Must you come here drunk?" he demanded. "Throw away your wine!"*

*"Oh no, sir!" she replied. "I haven't been
drinking wine or anything stronger. But I
am very discouraged, and I was pouring out
my heart to the Lord. Don't think I am a
wicked woman! For I have been praying out
of great anguish and sorrow." "In that case,"
Eli said, "go in peace! May the God of Israel
grant the request you have asked of him."*
(1 Samuel 1:10-17 NLT)

Hannah was desperate. She longed for a child, and year
after year, it wasn't happening. Her husband had another
wife, Peninah, who was having child after child while Hannah
wasn't able to get pregnant. Not only was this devastating, this
rival wife made fun of Hannah's barrenness and mocked her
repeatedly.

Can you imagine being Hannah? It would feel like you were
living with the enemy day in and day out with no reprieve. Her
husband didn't understand why she wasn't happy with just him
and why she was so devastated. But Hannah knew she was created to be a mother. She loved her husband and she loved being
a wife, but she also knew there was more in her to be lived
out. She longed to be called "Mom" and create family, a long-
held desire within her. She was desperate and at her end. She
couldn't take one more day of taunting, so she did what all of
us should do. She went to God and she cried out to Him. It was
the desperate cries and prayers of Hannah that the Lord heard,
and from there filled her womb. She gave birth to a son named

Samuel, who was destined for amazing things. Desperation isn't pretty, but it will often release the breakthrough you have been contending for!

Hannah's son, Samuel, grew up to become a prophet during a pivotal era in Israel's history. I love that Hannah's desperation produced a prophet, a mouthpiece of the Lord. When we go to God in the dark nights and difficult times, He hears our cries and knows our anguish. Our cries and prayers of desperation can lead to some of our greatest breakthroughs and testimonies. In one chapter, we see Hannah crying out to the Lord from a place of deep pain and disappointment, and at the end of that same chapter, we see Hannah giving birth to Samuel and dedicating him to the Lord. Just because you are in the midst of times of anguish and pain doesn't mean your story stops there. Like Hannah, God is still writing your story. Though "weeping may stay for the night, rejoicing comes in the morning" (Psalm 30:5b, NIV). With God, your story can change in a moment. One prayer, one encounter, one moment with Jesus and everything can change. Just like Hannah, keep going to God in the hard times. It is He who will see you through and fill your life with His blessings!

Remember, desperation doesn't have to be a bad thing. It just comes down to what it pulls out of you. Does it pull you into Jesus, moving you to lay everything down at His feet and surrender to His timing and His ways? Or does it pull you into striving and panic? The core of your driving force is essential to the fruit you will produce. Nothing good comes from stress, striving, and worry. How many times have I heard people say, even myself, "I wish I would have worried less and been present more"? When we worry, it removes us from key moments in our everyday life. Worry distracts you and disconnects you. It pulls you emotionally and mentally out of moments, causing you to obsess over things you often don't have control over. That is exhausting!

Have you ever noticed that when you are in a high-stress season, your sleep is affected as well as your emotional capacity? The enemy loves to wear us out by getting us focused on the obstacle in front of us, which causes us to lose sight that God has us. Stress is such a strategy of the enemy. When I'm stressed, I try to figure out the "why." Have I agreed to do too much? Have I put too much pressure on myself? Have I taken on other people's expectations that were never mine to carry? It could be all of those things or something else, but once we discover the source of stress, we need to ask the Lord for His wisdom. Are there things we can let go of and take off our plate? Is there a better way to do what is needed? Have we taken on things we don't need to? The Lord's perspective is greater than ours. Asking for His insight and viewpoint is so important. He can change our focus with one word, one encounter with Him. Throughout your journey of being single, consistently asking the Lord for His perspective will help guard your heart against hopelessness, anxiety, and discouragement.

When Christ isn't at the center of our desperation, it can cause us to make choices and decisions that we wouldn't normally make. Desperation that is not centered on Christ can lead us to unhealthy relationships and choices. That type of desperation isn't connected to hope. I don't know about you, but the times I have felt this the most, I haven't been very hopeful that the Lord was going to work things out for me. When I have felt desperate in my life, that is when I try to take matters into my own hands. I want to micromanage every part of the situation to ensure the result I want takes place. When we take control of the things we are supposed to leave in the Lord's hands, it can cause unnecessary messes. Being controlling never works out in the long run. Over time, it can sabotage relationships, complicate situations, and bring a lot of pain you didn't have to go through! How many times have we made situations in our lives harder than they needed to be, all because we didn't trust God and took matters into our own hands?

A guy I knew years ago was incredibly desperate to get married. He went on date after date trying to find Mrs. Right. Because I was friends with him, I was compelled to ask him why he was so determined to be in a relationship. I encouraged him to enjoy his season of singleness. For me, no one had captured my heart or attention, and settling wasn't an option. But he could not relate to what I was saying at all. He had a goal, and the goal was to be married by the time he graduated from college. I talked to him about removing timelines, but in simple terms, he was not having it. Soon, he found himself a girlfriend. He shared with me he wasn't super attracted to her, but that she "could work" for marriage. I encouraged him to be patient and wait for someone he was truly in love with. They both deserved that. I said I felt he was trying too hard to just make it work and find someone to marry. I'll never forget the look on his face. He looked at me like I was crazy and said he didn't have time to wait for all that. He wanted to be married after he graduated from college and the clock was ticking.

So many times we get weary in the waiting, so we begin to ignore when we feel a check or a lack of peace. We chalk it up to nerves or indigestion when actually, we just don't have peace and we know we should not be out with that person. Or we are just tired of being alone, so we ignore the warning signs and then justify the decision to do things our own way.

Like my friend, so many of us let the ticking clock drive us rather than our heart and the timing of the Lord. The infamous "clock" of life, whether it be biological or emotional, is real and is one of the most common detractors that can pull you from your place of peace and rest into striving and anxiety. The only way you don't let the "ticking clock" drive you is when you have the promise of the Lord to ground you. It is so easy to get swept up in how we think things should go, but having the promise of the Lord is what keeps us rooted in a place of peace and rest.

I have seen so many people get married young, excited about the idea of marriage, but not really understanding what they were signing up for, only to discover a couple years into marriage that it was not what they expected. Many of these couples end up in divorce court. This should serve as a sobering reminder that marriage is such a massive decision in our lives.

As excited as you are about the *idea* of getting married, understand that it is nothing that should be rushed into or forced. We should be encouraged to wait and not to settle for less than what is God-ordained.

I believe a lot of my resolve to wait for the man I believed was a "God match" for me came from the example my parents gave me. I was raised in a home with a happy marriage. My parents showed me the joy and fulfillment a marriage can give you. They laughed together constantly, giving me the understanding that friendship is the foundation to a solid union. Because I had the daily example of a good marriage, I was determined to wait for the right man at the right time. I remember, one time, receiving several dozen red roses from multiple men during a short period of time. It was a bit overwhelming and I was flattered that the guys were interested, but I had no peace to date any of them. I remember the Lord saying to me during that time, "Don't confuse flattery with My approval." So I waited.

Waiting for the Breakthrough

Scripture is riddled with people who had to wait for their breakthrough—Hannah, Ruth, Elijah, Moses, the children of Israel. And that's just to name a few. I've come to realize we are always going to be waiting for something. It's safe to say that if you're reading this book, you are likely waiting for the Lord to bring that special person into your life. But before you were waiting for your spouse, you were waiting for something else. And after you get married, you'll wait for other things. Truth is, you'll always be waiting for something, and because of this, it's so important that you truly grab hold of the significance of the "waiting seasons" of your life. The posture of our hearts is so critical during these times. What we meditate on and allow ourselves to fixate on is everything.

For me, it was not getting on the "What if" train I mentioned previously, ignoring the steady stream of worst-case scenarios that tempted me to fixate on things that could steal my contentment. These possibilities and questions can fill all of us with worry, concern, anxiety and stress! And what is crazy is that all of these scenarios aren't even reality!

When I am waiting and contending for a promise, what I allow my heart and mind to rest on is essential and connected to the state in which I will find myself. If I allow my mind to wander and accept any thought creeping in, I will find myself in a space that isn't residing in the peace and rest of the Lord. Instead, I will be like Elijah, hiding in a cave afraid and terrified! I always marvel at this story because it is such a picture of how you and I act at times in our own relationships with the Lord.

Elijah experienced one of the most epic displays of the power of God when he called down fire from heaven and wiped out eight-hundred-and-fifty false prophets. Elijah obeyed the instruction of the Lord and the false god Baal was exposed. Everyone acknowledged that the God of Elijah was the one true God! When Queen Jezebel heard what happened, she sent Elijah a death threat. Elijah was terrified, fled for his life, and ended up hiding in a cave. One day, he was possessed with the power of God and walking in the office of a prophet, destroying the false prophets of Baal, and the next day he was afraid and hiding from Jezebel. In twenty-four hours, Elijah went from having a front-row seat to an incredible demonstration of the power of God to fleeing for his life! What is crazy is that Elijah intimately knew how powerful God is! But fear overwhelmed him.

I have had experiences just like this. One day, I'm preaching and standing in the midst of the presence of God. I am steady in my confidence, bold as a lion, and I feel every bit of God's power and authority. I am unwavering, standing in sheer confidence in who my King is. The next day, I get bad news, or the enemy comes with his onslaught of warfare, and I find myself running and hiding. My identity in Christ is nowhere to be found, until the Lord finds me hiding like Elijah and asks me, "Christa, what are you doing here?"

It's when I hear His voice that everything clicks back into place. When I hear His voice, I'm reminded of who I am, and hiding is not who I am. I am a child of God and my weapons are my worship and my praise. I will not be weighed down by things I cannot control, but I will rise above and focus on Who is in control, even when things feel out of control.

Hiding is not who you are. You have nothing to fear, nothing to shrink back from. Your heavenly Father is the Great I Am. No weapon formed against you can prosper. The Lord will never leave you or forsake you. When I need to be reminded of who my God is, I go through His names, because whatever I need in that moment is found in one of His names. I find so much peace in the fact that whatever I am facing, He is the answer. There is nothing that is too big for Him or that surprises Him. He is all-knowing, ever-present, and always faithful.

So much of warfare is definitely about our perspective. If the enemy can distort our perspective on who God is and His character, then he can often get us to believe a lie. Bill Johnson said this one time and it forever impacted me: "If you don't have hope in every area of your life, it means you've believed a lie somewhere along the way." Selah. Meditate on that for a moment. If you do not have hope in *every* area of your life, that means the enemy has distorted who God is in that area. Because God is hope, we should have hope for every area of our lives. That hope quiets down all of our doubts and worries, keeps us off of the "What if" train, and allows us to rest in Him. (For more on the Names of God, refer to the Addendum at the end of the book.)

Hebrews 4 talks about a *rest* that is available to all those who believe. The Lord has reserved a rest for His sons and daughters, and it is rooted in our covenant with Him. We can rest and trust in the goodness of the Lord. Rest is trusting God. Trusting God breaks striving and worry, allowing us to enter into a place of rest that is bigger than what we feel or what is going on around us. Rest is the quiet confidence of knowing and believing God does not deny His Word, and therefore, His promises will come to pass.

It is through our Christ-centered desperation that Jesus can create in us a depth in our relationship with Him that few other things can. It has been my personal moments of desperation that have unlocked depths of intimacy with Jesus I don't think would have come if I had gone any other way. Even when this season of your life ends, you will be able to look back at these moments and realize these are the seasons that made you who you are.

The Art of Waiting in Desperate Times

Here are three ways to combat desperation when it comes knocking:

1. **Keep your focus on the big picture.** Your current place in life is temporary, and even though you may be years deep into it, it doesn't mean it's your life sentence. Desperate thinking makes you lose sight of the bigger picture. One way to combat desperate thinking is to fill your life with things you are passionate about! When you have things in your life that are exciting and give you joy, it then gives you purpose, which helps keep you connected to the bigger picture.

2. **Don't allow fear to be your driving force.** When we get desperate, we often get afraid things aren't going to change or that God isn't going to come through. Desperation feeds on fear. Don't feed the fear by giving into it. You reject fear by daily spending time with the Lord and being intentional about

deepening your walk with Him. Get in the Word and know what He says about you and the promises that come from the covenant we have with Him. When I spend time with God, it always grounds me and shifts my perspective when my focus needs a realignment. Fear will try to bait you to settle and lower your standards in who you date. Don't give into the fear. Although my journey of waiting lasted nineteen years, when my husband Sean came into my life, I was so glad I didn't settle! He was so worth the wait! Know your worth and value, and punch fear in the face!

3. **Don't remove the God factor.** When we are desperate, we can easily get sucked into thinking the breakthrough depends on us, when it actually depends on God. Don't take on false responsibility. The enemy would love to get you bogged down, thinking if you were at the right place at the right time, then you'd meet the love of your life. Or if you looked a certain way, weighed a certain amount, said the right thing, and so on. You are not perfect, and if the Lord brings someone into your life, you need to realize they will not be perfect either. This isn't about perfection, it's about being yourself. God is the One who will do this. You don't have to make it happen. I think when we are desperate, it's easy to want to start manipulating and controlling in

order to create as many opportunities as possible. Hear what I am saying. Live your life. Be present. Make friends. Be a part of an awesome community of believers. Meet people and walk through open doors. But understand that this is about trusting God and watching Him write your story, not taking the pen out of His hand and writing your own.

ZERO IN ON:

➤ Desperation isn't pretty, but it will often release the breakthrough you have been contending for!

➤ Just because you are in the midst of times of anguish and pain doesn't mean your story stops there.

➤ One prayer, one encounter, one moment with Jesus and everything can change.

➤ The only way you don't let the "ticking clock" drive you is when you have the promise of the Lord to ground you.

07

BREAKING THE STIGMA OF SINGLENESS

Being single isn't a curse! Let's just establish that right now. If you never get married, you are not cursed or undesirable. Being married or unmarried doesn't affect your value or worth. We can all agree God can and will do incredible things in your life whether you are single, married, divorced, or widowed. Your relationship status doesn't change you in the eyes of the Lord! You are loved and valued no matter what. Being single can be a gift and a time to grow and mature as a person.

A mindset I often came up against was that singleness is a curse. People often approached me like I had done something wrong or missed the guy along the way and that's why I was single. When I was in my twenties, I actually had a well-known leader and pastor in the body of Christ interrupt me during a worship service and say, "I don't get it. I don't get why you're single. You're attractive and you love God. You must sabotage relationships with men. You must have men issues and that's why you're single." After dumping his conclusion on me, he walked away and went back to worshiping God. I stood there stunned, hurt, and dumbfounded that he would say that to me. I've always thought of myself as someone who values men and has really great relationships with men. I was blessed to be raised by an incredibly kind father, who loved me completely and who I always felt very cherished and celebrated by. So, for this pastor to come to me and say he thought the reason I was single was because I had men issues brought so much confusion! Because we all have blind spots in our lives, I wasn't sure if this was a blind spot moment for me. This interaction caused me a lot of pain and doubt.

The rest of the weekend, I carried this statement with me, feeling deflated and confused. I called my dad, told him what had happened, and asked him to be honest and tell me if there was any truth to the statement. I needed to know if there was something in me that was sabotaging relationships with men and that was why I was still single in my mid-twenties. My dad assured me that I did not sabotage relationships with men, and that he had never seen any behavior or attitude in me other than love and appreciation for men. He encouraged me that what that person said wasn't true, and that I shouldn't worry about it and just move on.

I tried, but the person's words kept lingering. During that time in my life, I was the director of a school of ministry, so

I was on staff at a church. The following Monday morning, I walked into my senior pastor's office and asked if I could have a minute. I shared with him what had been spoken over me and asked for honest feedback if he saw any truth in this. He assured me that he hadn't seen anything in me that didn't honor, value, or respect men. He then went on to say he didn't agree with what had been spoken and that I just needed to let it go.

Here is what is crazy to me. I was only twenty-six years old when that happened. Little did I know it would still be another thirteen years before I got married. I didn't comprehend it at the time, but I learned a key lesson through that whole situation. I learned that when you respect and look up to someone, their voice has a lot of weight in your life. If you aren't careful, you can take their interpretation of your situation as your truth when it is merely their perspective and not necessarily God's. Now, please hear me. I believe in people speaking into my life and having consistent accountability, but there are also times when people who love you will speak things over you that are not truth.

Because what had been spoken was from someone I valued and respected, I had a really hard time letting it go. Although I don't believe it was the intention of the person who spoke it, what they said left a residue of hopelessness over me and it needed to be broken off! I had to spend several days with the Lord, wrestling through this whole situation. Finally, the Lord spoke to me and said, "Christa, he simply does not understand why you are single. And because he doesn't understand, he has created a reason that makes sense to him. It's not true. You do not have issues with men. This is him trying to understand what he doesn't understand. Let go of people's opinions and conclusions of why they think you're single. You're single because I have kept you single."

Freedom! When the Lord spoke that to my heart, it truly set me free and His peace and confidence washed over me. The reason I was single was because the Lord had hidden me in this area, and it wasn't His time yet. I hadn't done anything wrong. I didn't sabotage relationships with men. I didn't have men issues. It was simply because God hadn't released me into that season. When other people do not understand your process or circumstances, they will create their own, sometimes wrong, conclusions to create an explanation they are comfortable with.

When the Lord showed me this, the confusion I had been battling for days broke off! I wasn't angry or upset with the person, and I was able to let it go. In that encounter, I realized it wasn't my responsibility to make people understand my journey with the Lord, because honestly, it had nothing to do with them. How freeing is that?

Now, I want to bring some balance to what I am sharing right now. There are times in our lives where people may say some things to us we don't want to hear, and although we may not like the package or appreciate the source it came through, we need to remain teachable, humble, and willing to receive constructive feedback. Even when it's hard, I think it's important we stay open. We are works in progress *and* process. Like

Paul says, daily we have to work out our own salvation with fear and trembling:

> *Therefore, my beloved, as you have always obeyed, not as in my presence only, but now much more in my absence, work out your own salvation with fear and trembling; for it is God who works in you both to will and to do for His good pleasure.* (Philippians 2:12-13 NKJV)

This means that daily, you and I come in reverence and in awe to the Creator of the heavens and the earth, recognizing we need Him to work in us and through us. It is only through His Spirit that we are able to be transformed into looking, loving, and being like Him. When many people read this Scripture, they get tripped up with the word "fear," but this isn't saying God wants us to be afraid of Him. The fear Paul is talking about here isn't connected with anxiety or panic—it's referring to a reverence for God. We need to understand there is an attitude and posture of awe and wonder we should have with the Lord. He created the heavens and earth. He created the human body and the human race. Every star you see, He created. He designed the oceans and the animals and the terrain of the world. When you begin to think about just how awesome and amazing He is, it naturally pulls out the awe of the wonder of our incredible God!

In comparison to Him, we are very human and very weak. Without Christ, we can do nothing, but through Him we are moving from glory to glory, being made into His likeness. That means there are areas in your life that still need work, and that's okay. It doesn't necessarily mean that an area of lack is your fault or because you've done something wrong. It simply means that our lives are submitted to the Lordship of Christ, and if there is something that hasn't "happened" yet, that's on God, not on us. It is not a flippant or uncaring attitude. It is, once again, about taking a position of trust and surrender. And if there is an area that needs oversight and correction, the Holy Spirit is faithful to let us know. That's also where trusted advisors and mentors like my parents and my pastor come in. Know the people who are for you. These are the ones who have done the time with you and are therefore able to speak lovingly and honestly into your life. These are the ones who will affirm your decision to trust the Lord with everything and encourage your pursuit of God's best.

Staying consistent in your pursuit can make you weary, so you need to be surrounded by words and people that keep you lifted. It is not a physical weariness—it is spiritual, emotional, and mental weariness, which I find way more exhausting than anything physical. You and I won't wait long if we do it by sheer will, because waiting requires a supernatural grace and support of the Holy Spirit.

In 1 Corinthians, Paul shows us the value of being single. In your singleness you have less things taking up your time. You aren't having to take care of a spouse and fewer things are pulling on your attention. I know you may be thinking, *I want the distraction of marriage!* I get it, I truly do. But this whole journey is about you getting to a place of surrendering marriage to the Lord and trusting Him with your story. It's also about changing your perspective and mindset on how you view your singleness. Paul writes this:

> *I want you to live as free of complications as possible. When you're unmarried, you're free to concentrate on simply pleasing the Master. Marriage involves you in all the nuts and bolts of domestic life and in wanting to please your spouse, leading to so many more demands on your attention. The time and energy that married people spend on caring for and nurturing each other, the unmarried can spend in becoming whole and holy instruments of God. I'm trying to be helpful and make it as easy as possible for you, not make things harder. All I want is for you to be able to develop a way of life in which you can spend plenty of time together with the Master without a lot of distractions.*
> (1 Corinthians 7:32-35 MSG)

I love this portion of Scripture and often meditated on it during my waiting season. When the waiting became a burden,

I went back to this and, once again, put my desire for marriage back into the hands of the Lord. I wanted my life to be solely focused on Him. I didn't want to waste my single years vying for something I wasn't sure was going to happen. I knew as I spent more time with the Lord, perspective and peace would follow. Like Paul said, let us live a life as free of complications and distractions as possible. This isn't easy and takes a daily surrender to the Lord. How many times did I give the Lord my desire to be married? Countless! This isn't a one-time thing. This cycle takes place again and again until it's done.

Here's the truth. Some people would actually be less distracted being single, but there are also some who would be less distracted being married. Everyone's wired differently. But I love how Paul just keeps it real. When you are married, there is a division of your time and attention. It's true. It's not bad, but your time and your life are no longer just yours. When you get married, you are sharing your life fully with another person. Paul, of course, isn't saying marriage is a bad thing—he's simply saying this is the reality of marriage. Then he goes on to highlight a benefit of being single. You don't have divided time and attention. It is much easier being single to give yourself fully to God.

Although our society may put greater value on those who are in a relationship and/or married, God doesn't. You are not living this life for anyone else—you are living it for Jesus. Other people don't have to understand your process, you just have to be confident in yours. And when you feel like you are wavering, look to God and push through whatever is trying to hold you back.

Let me take a moment and speak honestly into *your* life. I want to empower you in your season so that you won't be hindered from receiving what the Lord has for you even now. Let's remove some of the things you may hear or experience that try to derail you from engaging authentically in your season of singleness. Because the struggle is real, so real. In my years of being single, there were many days I had to push through my stuff, but also there were days I had to push through the stuff other people tried putting on me.

Pushing Through Others' Opinions

Before I turned thirty-five, I often heard people say, "He's coming. You're going to be married. It's going to be great." Post-thirty-five, people started asking me, "Do you even want to get married?" Their comments fully shifted from faith-filled encouragement to, "Is this really going to happen?" For them, the impossibilities grew the older I became. I even had someone share an old article from *Newsweek* with me that declared single women over 40 are more likely to be killed by terrorism than get married. That was actually published! Lord, please help people in their ignorance!

You may have had similar experiences. The well-meaning, but sometimes careless, words of others can often feed our insecurities and make us doubt the timing of God. These are the moments we have to be intentional about speaking the truth of God to combat any lies we are tempted to agree with. One of my favorite truths is a verse that is recited a lot. Sometimes it's the ones we often repeat and allow to become our anthems that are the most life-giving. The following verse found in Proverbs has become that verse for me:

> *Trust in the Lord with all your heart and lean not on your own understanding; in all your ways submit to him, and he will make your paths straight.* (Proverbs 3:5-6 NIV)

Simple, but profound, if we live it out. Life-changing, if we activate it in our lives.

When I was wrestling with that pastor's comments that I must have issues with men, the words the Lord spoke to me about other people's lack of understanding and releasing other people's opinions lifted such a heavy weight. I always want to be someone who is teachable and accountable, which is why I went to my dad and my pastor when this was initially spoken over me. I wanted to make sure there was no truth in what was said. We are not always the most objective when it comes to taking inventory of ourselves. But hearing my pastor and my dad confirm that those words were not true was very encouraging. At my core, I knew it wasn't true, but I was grateful to get confirmation. Through that whole experience, I realized even though people care about you and they want what is best for you, it doesn't mean they will always understand you. Being understood by those who love you isn't always a guarantee and that's okay. It doesn't mean they can't pray for you and stand with you believing for God's promises. It just means you have to be wise in what you allow to be spoken over you and what words you receive as truth.

Years later, I did go back to that leader to share with him how his words hurt me. You know what was crazy? He didn't even remember saying that! What may be very damaging for you may not even receive a second thought from the one who delivered the message. Why is this so important? Because there will be people who will come to conclusions and beliefs about why you are single or what you should be doing in your journey of singleness. They may tell you what you are doing wrong and try to convince you that is the reason for your singleness. I encourage you to be wise about what you accept as truth. Go to the spiritual leaders in your life and ask for feedback and counsel. Everyone has an opinion, but the Lord's opinion is the highest and really matters. He is the One you should ultimately lean on and the One who will make your paths straight before Him.

Also, be a person who surrounds yourself with people who are rooted and grounded in His Word and Spirit. When the Lord speaks or He uses them to speak into your life, you can trust it. I want you to be empowered in your journey of singleness. People will often project their life experiences (both positive and negative) on you, with the intent to spare you the pain they went through, not realizing by doing so they can begin to limit and/or distort the story God is writing through you.

Pushing Through Unanswered Prayers

When I was in college, I had the biggest crush on this guy. If I'm being honest, it was probably more like borderline infatuation. I was convinced I was going to marry him. He and I became good friends and hung out all the time. This did not help my heart. The more we hung out, the deeper in "like" I fell. At the time, I thought he was confident, super cool, and independent. In retrospect, he was arrogant, elitist, and aloof. Funny how the heart can skew the reality of who someone is showing you they are. He would make fun of me when we hung out, but I made excuses for him, believing that he felt really comfortable with me and could show me his true self. I took his teasing as a compliment. Even though he put me down, I always felt the need to prove I was cool enough to hang out with him. As I look back, I know that he was actually showing me his true self. He wasn't that kind and definitely was not connected to my heart.

For an entire school year, I was infatuated with him. He talked about other girls with me, and I kept thinking that at any time he was going to realize I was the girl of his dreams! It never happened. What did happen was that after summer break, I found out that he was dating . . . you guessed it, my friend who lived across the hall. Yes, this is the guy I mentioned earlier in the book. Honestly, it was brutal. But something good did come out of it. It pushed me back into the lap of Jesus. In time, the Lord began to take off the blinders around how I saw this guy. He wasn't a bad guy, but he clearly was not a God match for me. I remember praying so many times for the Lord to change this guy's heart and for him to realize I was the girl for him! But thankfully that didn't happen. God loves me and wanted the best for me, so He didn't answer that prayer.

Sometimes we become so blindsided by our feelings and distorted perceptions that we are convinced that a certain person must be God's will for our life when they aren't. We make excuses for their behavior and ignore the times they make us feel less-than, convincing ourselves this is God's will. Then, when it doesn't happen, we get offended at God, when what He is actually doing is protecting us! Don't get offended when God doesn't answer your prayers. It just may be the protection of the Lord. You're not just waiting for someone to finally pick you! Recognize your value and worth and what you bring to the table, because *you* are incredible. Ask yourself, "Does this situation or this person really make me feel cherished and valued?" It has to be a two-way street. That's real relationship.

When I reflect back on that time in my life and think about what would have happened if God *had* answered that prayer, I realize how different my life would have been. I would not be who I am today or have the experiences I've had if I'd married him. But God saw that. God sees the big picture. When doors close or when people are not interested in you, you can trust that God sees the whole picture and His understanding overrides your lack of it.

When all of that happened, I was heartbroken, and the pain was real. But as time passed, my perspective shifted and I began to see what God saw. This guy didn't see me as special or someone he wanted to spend the rest of his life with. If another person does not have feelings for you, accept it. Don't try to prove them wrong and convince them you are worth their time and attention. If you have to convince them, you'll have to keep convincing them. You need to be with someone who values and celebrates you, someone who celebrates your strengths and doesn't exploit your weaknesses. If you have to prove you are worth someone's time, then they are not worth your time. People who love you should already see your value without you needing to convince them of it.

It is very easy to know if someone is a good fit for you simply by seeing (and being honest) about how they treat you. Even if there is a lot of attraction and chemistry between the two of you, attraction and chemistry do not equal a God-centered relationship. You want someone you feel safe with, who believes in you and gets you! If you are not feeling that at the friendship level, then you are not going to experience that in a romantic relationship with them. Allow friendship to be a guide to discover who that person really is. How they treat you as a friend is a window into how they will treat you in a relationship and marriage. Friendship is the foundation of a great marriage. So if they don't treat you well as a friend, you will not have a great marriage.

Unanswered prayers are sometimes our greatest blessings!

Pushing Through the Timelines of Others

We create timelines off of social norms and structures. None of these timelines created by society are based on heaven's timeline over our lives—they are based on what we've learned and been taught is "normal." But who says that has to be the norm? It definitely was not my normal. I felt like as the years went by, I was being given the opportunity to create a new normal for single people through my own story. I wanted to remove the timeline of society off myself and off others. I wanted to challenge the thinking that certain things have to happen by a certain time. I wanted to see God get out of the box we often put Him in! I encourage you to do the same. Break down the boxes that timelines put you in. Who says you have to be married in your twenties or thirties? Who says you have to date a bunch of different people to know who the "one" is? Jesus never said any of these things. Jesus simply said, "Follow Me and love Me with undivided attention and affection. Give your life completely to me." Those are the instructions of the Lord, not the timelines that we have conditioned ourselves to live by. By breaking down boxes that constrain and restrict God, we then agree to Him being the Author of our story and not a predisposed timeline society boxes us into. I want you to have the freedom to be different and live by a different timeline that the Lord is writing through your life. Don't be constrained by something society has created that doesn't have the fingerprint of heaven.

Some of the hardest things I had to lay down again and again were my own personal timelines and expectations. There is a certain way each of us envisions our lives turning out. We all have quiet, unspoken ideas about where we will be in our twenties, thirties, forties, and beyond. When our expected timeline isn't being lived out, it can cause a lot of anxiety, stress, and disillusionment. That is when it is so easy to start looking around and seeing other people live out what we thought we would at a certain time, and it is in that moment we have to not only lay down the idea of being married, but also our timing and expectations.

Pushing through others' expectations is also something I didn't expect to have to do, but like everything else, I had to lay them down. I had to lay down what other people were putting on me. People who loved me, prayed for me, and stood with me, believing for the promises of God to come to pass in my life had their own expectations and opinions as to when they believed I would be married. When those years came and went, I saw the disappointment on their faces. Although their motives and intentions for me were sincere and good, I realized I struggled with disappointing people. I did not want to let down the ones I knew were praying and standing with me. So when prophetic words were not fulfilled and timelines were not met, I had to let go of the false responsibility and realize I wasn't the one that could answer prayers! Only God could do that! Don't own what is not your responsibility!

Everyone who loves you has a certain opinion on when your various milestones should take place. It's not necessarily a bad thing, but it can cause unnecessary stress and anxiety when you take on what you're not supposed to carry. Because we have all been raised in a society where there are certain expectations for when you should get married, people close to us can unknowingly succumb to the false belief system of conditioned timelines for your life. So I am going to say again what I said just a moment ago. The timelines of society are not the timelines of heaven. As you are in the process of pushing through the stuff, recognize that this simply means laying down the challenges and the hardships throughout your journey of singleness and trusting God fully. Pushing through = trusting Him.

Pushing Through Other People's Experiences

Regardless of current relationship status, each person has experiences in the area of the heart. Some of those experiences are good and some of those experiences are not so good. And believe me, you will be bombarded with various versions of relational tales. People often want to share their stories with you for two reasons: 1) They think how they did it was right, so they want you to do the same, and 2) They think they did it wrong and want you to avoid what they went through. As we receive the experiences of others, so many times we are then tasked with sifting through the life lessons of others.

When one of my sisters was about to give birth to her first child, I was often amused at the number of women who stopped her when we were out in public to tell her what she needed to do to help induce labor. They would share the last thing they were doing before they went into labor. My sister and I would laugh, because many of these women believed that whatever they were doing right before they went into labor was the thing that caused them to go into labor, when in all actuality, it just happened to be the thing they were doing right before they went into labor. Because these women thought they had an inside scoop for my sister, they felt compelled to share with her how to induce her labor.

The same goes for people with their stories of meeting a spouse. Many people will tell you exactly what they did right before they met their husband or wife, and they are convinced that is the secret ingredient to landing a spouse. In all actuality, it may have simply been the timing of the Lord for them to meet that person—if they didn't manipulate or control the situation (I'm smiling as I write that). People are quick to give you their advice and inside strategies to help you find that someone special. Even with their good intentions, they will share what they think is coveted information, in hopes you will repeat what they did in your own life. I rarely found this to be helpful, because all it did was cause me, once again, to have to push through everyone's expectations and timelines as to how and when I should meet my husband.

On the other side of this scenario is people telling you everything they did wrong and how they are now either divorced, heartbroken, or in a loveless marriage. They are determined to share with you to spare you the pain they went through or are currently going through. They then give you a list of dos and don'ts from their story, which doesn't apply to yours. That is their experience, but that doesn't mean it will be your experience. Don't take on other people's disappointments and negative relationships. Push through.

This is what I want you to walk away with. I want you to know that you are living a story only you can live. Recognize that your journey and life experiences will be different than those around you. Although there might be similarities here and there, at the end of the day, this is about you living fully and completely for God. You need to recognize that the story of love in your life begins with Jesus and everything else comes out of that relationship with Him. Pushing through everyone's stuff is simply pushing into God. No matter how many times you have to do this and lay stuff down, let it always lead you back to the feet of Jesus, resting and trusting. God has your story in His timeline, and in His own way, He will bring things to pass.

Pushing Through Moments That Don't Look Like How You Expected

When I was in my mid-twenties, I went overseas to attend a well-known school of ministry. I had already graduated from college and had been working in the fashion industry for a couple of years. During this time, I discovered I had a passion for preaching and ministry. I resigned my position in the fashion industry and moved halfway around the world to go through the pastoral ministry program of this school of ministry. Before leaving for this God adventure, I received several prophetic words about how this time would be a launchpad for me and the ministry I carry. I received prophetic words saying I would be preaching to rooms full of people and that I had a voice that was meant to be heard. I was excited and expectant as I got on that plane for this next chapter of my life. But, when I arrived, I quickly realized the program I had signed up for wasn't about getting me ready for a platform ministry. Instead, it was about preparing me to serve the people of God, win souls, and disciple new Christians.

I didn't realize how much I needed these fundamentals in my Christian walk. Prior to going through this program, I served in the youth ministry of my local church for years. I also enjoyed sharing my faith at work and seeing God move in the secular work arena. But I can't say I understood the joy of serving, nor was I passionate for lost souls or discipling those who had given their lives to Jesus. I had grown so accustomed to the "evangelism" department of the church that I didn't really know how to do discipleship. This program was so good for me, because it got my eyes off myself and focused on how I could love and serve those around me.

Of course, learning any lesson and truth in life is often a process, and me learning how to serve was definitely a journey. Over the course of one eye-opening weekend, God showed me how to fully understand this truth. For this particular weekend, the church had invited a man who moved mightily in the prophetic ministry and healing to come and speak. I was so excited to attend this service and sit under this person's ministry. A few days before this highly anticipated weekend, the school administration announced that all the students were being assigned to departments where they would be serving for the whole weekend. Because I was in the Pastoral Ministry program, I assumed I would be a greeter, usher, or altar worker. What I did not expect was to be assigned to the nursery. Wait, what? Nursery? I thought they had it wrong. I was called to preach, to minister, and to prophesy. I could work the altars, give prophetic words to the people, and pray for the sick. I rationalized how I would be utilized much better *in* the service and not serving downstairs in the nursery with no connection to what was happening in the sanctuary. I immediately tried to think of ways I could get out of serving in the nursery and attend the services!

Before you start judging me and thinking I am a horrible person for not wanting to be in the nursery, I ask you to extend me some grace. I love kids, they are amazing, but I wanted to be equipped and prepared for the ministry I believed the Lord had called me to. My twenty-something-year-old perspective didn't understand how working in the nursery would actually help that. Being the assertive woman I am (my husband is laughing right now), I went to the person over our assignments, explained my gift mix and what I am called to do, and said I didn't think serving in the nursery was going to help develop that call in my life. They smiled and said, "It will help develop the call." I knew there was no way out and I was so frustrated. I did not want to miss out on the services, and I did not want to have to hear about how awesome it was while I was stuck down in the basement with kids.

The service came and I dragged my heels as I reported to the nursery. I stood at the doorway of the sanctuary, peering in, desiring so badly to be in that room, until I felt a tap on my shoulder. The director of the nursery had come to look for me since I was late to check in. I quickly followed her, dejected that I had to miss the service. It was all I could think about. At times, I could even hear the roar of the people shouting and clapping over what the Lord was doing. All these little kids were around me, and all I could focus on was what I was missing.

The service went long that night, and as the time passed, I found myself playing with one little girl. Then the Lord spoke to me and said, "This is your ministry right now. This child."

I was surprised. "I'm called to preach and to minister to your people, Lord," I responded.

He said, "This is the gospel, Christa. This is your opportunity to live the gospel right now and love this child. Give her your best, your full attention and love. By doing that, you are preaching the gospel and ministering to my people. Her family is able to receive because you are taking care of their little girl. Don't underestimate the impact you are making in this moment. This is ministry. This is my gospel. Love the one in front of you."

Mic drop.

Wait, what? How was working in the nursery connected in any way to me preaching the gospel and being a voice for my generation? Because it is bigger than me and it is bigger than you. It's about loving people *every* day in the mundane, predictable, ordinary moments of life. These moments are God wooing us to press beyond the obvious details of the moment and go deeper.

All of a sudden, I was filled with love and joy for this little girl. I fully engaged with her and enjoyed my time with her. I began to play with the other children, holding them, laughing with them, dancing with them, and valuing them just like Jesus would. My mindset completely shifted from what I was missing to what I was privileged to give to these little ones. They weren't the reason I wasn't in the adults meeting that evening, but the assignment God had given me. They were sponges for love and affection.

Something shifted in me that night. The push to be at the right table or in the right meeting or to be connected to the right people broke off of me. When the Lord spoke to my heart that night about living the gospel and loving the one in front of me, everything became clear. Everything I was concerned about didn't really matter to Jesus. What mattered to Jesus was His kids being loved well.

I share this story to encourage you to lean into the moments that make up your season of waiting. You may be asked to do something that seems so contrary to what you are waiting and believing for. This is not the burden-inducing expectations of others but the times when the Lord asks you to be faithful in an area that may not make sense. But you never know what you are being asked to do that not only impacts His kingdom but also prepares you for what you are praying for. Being faithful in the small and even hidden areas of your life positions you to reap well in the areas to come.

Pushing Through Weariness in the Midst of Delay

I know what it is to wait for things. Waiting nineteen years is a long time, and one thing I came to understand during almost two decades of waiting is that when promises and breakthroughs are delayed, it makes us very vulnerable and susceptible to disillusionment, offense, and compromise. The longer we wait, the more tempted we are to compromise and ease up on our moral convictions and standards.

Here's the thing we have to understand. If you're about God's business, He will be about yours. During the latter part of my nineteen years of waiting, this truth became a greater place of resolve within me. When I found myself weary, tempted to lower my standards and settle for what I knew wasn't God's best, I would go back and read the prophetic words I had received about my calling and my destiny. I would meditate on the life Scriptures the Lord had given me when I had sought Him, and I would pour myself into what I had in my hand at that time in my life, whether I was working a mundane job or a job I loved. I found something or someone to pour into that would get my eyes off myself. For me, when I'm fighting through disappointment, it helps when I do a creative project in my home because I love interior design. Or I plan a fun adventure with a friend that will get my focus off my troubles and get me laughing and enjoying my life! There were many times I found myself feeling restless with my singleness, so I'd organize a girls' night hangout or a movie night at my house. Fill your life with fun, community, and things you are passionate about. Cultivate laughter and joy. I still do this. If I wake up and I'm feeling heavy, I'll spend time with the Lord and then I'll figure out a way to do something that day that brings me joy, whether small or big.

What you don't want to do is allow the *weariness* of waiting to chip away at your *resolve* in waiting for God's best:

> *Let us not become weary in doing good, for*
> *at the proper time we will reap a harvest if*
> *we do not give up.* (Galatians 6:9 NIV)

When we get weary and our lives feel dull, boring, and mundane, we look for adventure and inspiration. If we aren't rooted in trusting and communing with God, we will find counterfeit fulfillment in places and people that are not the Lord's best for us. It becomes easier to lower our standards and make someone "spouse material" when in all actuality, they aren't. You're just tired of waiting. Don't let weariness be your decision maker.

Recognizing how you respond in those moments of weariness is essential in how you walk out your journey. The journey to be content yet contending for the promises of God over your life is not easy. If it were, then so many people wouldn't settle for an Ishmael version of what they have been believing for. Remember Abraham and Sarah? They got tired of waiting for the promised child, so they made it happen themselves and made a mess that affected generations! But when we wait on God to fulfill His Word in His timing, then it will be His best! That is what we want—*His* best, not our version of it!

None of us can wait on God through sheer willpower. It must be through the Holy Spirit sustaining us and giving us the grace to wait. We were never created to do this alone. We must invite the Holy Spirit into our journey. Invite Holy Spirit into the great days and the hard days. He's got you. Surround yourself with people who constantly point you towards Jesus and speak His truth to you, reminding you of what the Lord has spoken over you! To this day, I ask my husband, family, and close friends to "speak truth" over me when I am overcome with the delays of life. They tell me again and again what God has said over me. They remind me of the prophetic words I have received and speak hope and life to my situation! Every time they do this, I feel a divine exchange take place. I feel Jesus take the heaviness and leave me with His peace. When I hear truth, it always brings alignment back to my spirit and puts my heart and mind at ease. His Word and His promises are always the place we must come back to:

> *The minute I said, "I'm slipping, I'm fall-*
> *ing," your love, God, took hold and held me*
> *fast. When I was upset and beside myself,*
> *you calmed me down and cheered me up.*
> (Psalm 94:18-19 MSG)

When anxiety wants to creep in, shut the door on it by declaring *God's truth* over yourself! I can't count how many times I've slathered some olive oil on my own self and prayed in the Holy Ghost! I know that when I call His name and commune with the Holy Spirit, the lies of the enemy always get exposed and broken. Don't accept what the enemy is throwing at you. You have the Spirit of God living inside of you. Access Him and enforce the blood covenant of Jesus Christ.

ZERO IN ON:

➤ **Other people don't have to understand your process. You just have to be confident in yours.**

➤ **People who love you should already see your value. You don't need to convince them of it.**

➤ **You need to recognize that the story of love in your life begins with Jesus and everything else comes out of that relationship with Him.**

➤ **Pushing through everyone's stuff is simply pushing into God.**

➤ **You never know what you are being asked to do that not only impacts His kingdom, but also prepares you for what you are praying for.**

08

NO MORE
BAGGAGE

In my years of ministry, I have counseled people in many walks of life, and I've come to realize that one of the hardest things for people to come to terms with is reconciling their life before Jesus to where they are currently. Maybe that is you reading this book right now. I want you to know that I have seen God heal people over and over again from their past and truly set them free! I've seen shame and bondage broken off through one encounter with the love of God! I've seen women who were once prostitutes now happily married and being incredible moms living for Jesus. I have seen the addicted, sexually deviant, and morally corrupt encounter Jesus and become a whole new person! Through Jesus, it's absolutely possible to be completely healed from your past:

> *This means that anyone who belongs to*
> *Christ has become a new person. The old life*

is gone; a new life has begun! (2 Corinthians
5:17 NLT)

When Jesus Christ is your Lord and Savior, you *are* a *new*
creation! You are no longer who you were before you surrendered to Jesus. I love how the footnote for 2 Corinthians in
The Passion Translation explains what it means when Scripture
talks about us becoming a new creation in Christ Jesus:

> This would include our old identity, our
> life of sin, the power of Satan, the reli-
> gious works of trying to please God, our
> old relationship with the world, and our
> old mind-sets. We are not reformed or
> simply refurbished, we are made com-
> pletely new by our union with Christ
> and the indwelling of the Holy Spirit.[4]

You are not just refurbished, you are completely new! That
is the power of the blood of Jesus! When you came into covenant with Jesus, you asked Him to forgive you of your sins. He
forgave you in that moment of confession. As you repented,
you severed your agreement with your past and asked Jesus to
cover your sins with His blood; therefore, all is washed clean
and forgiven.

---

[4] The Passion Translation Copyright © 2017, 2018 by Passion & Fire Ministries,
Inc. ThePassionTranslation.com.

So many people struggle with reconciling the lives they lived before they came into relationship with Jesus because, although they know Jesus has forgiven them, they haven't forgiven themselves. Allow your past to be something you learn from, but don't allow yourself to continue to be defined by it. It is behind you, completely removed from who you are today! Jesus died on the cross so that sin was defeated—*your* sin too. Don't allow the enemy to torment or harass you with things that don't belong to you anymore!

As singles walk out the waiting seasons of life, I always encourage them to use these seasons to work through their stuff. This is something I absolutely did in my own life. That doesn't mean when we get married we stop growing, but pursuing wholeness and healing in your life is a key component during your single years because it sets you up for the years to come. Part of our inheritance as sons and daughters of God is to live out the sanctified and authentic version of who Jesus created us to be. We should all want our full inheritance!

As a single person, you have this opportunity now. Sometimes we can look at our time of singleness as a filler season, thinking there is no deep work that needs to be done during it. It's not a filler season. It's an opportunity to build a strong foundation between you and the Lord. If you want to build an abundant life, a life where you are content, happy, and satisfied, that can only be done with Jesus as your foundation. If you want a healthy marriage, it can only happen if you are spiritually and emotionally whole and healed. What we don't deal with in our lives will often deal with us in the long run. This season is your opportunity to allow Jesus to fill in all the cracks in your foundation. This is your opportunity to allow God to get in there and bulldoze some false belief systems, destructive behaviors, and mindsets so that you can get healed, healthy, and whole! Wouldn't you rather make a decision about who you're going to marry from a healthy place rather than a broken one?

I know we are all busy and so many things are vying for our attention and time, but whatever your priorities are is what you will make time for. If spending time with God is a priority, then you'll make the time. If getting healed and healthy is your priority, then you'll make the time. Right now, you have the time to pursue God without interruption and without the natural pull of married life. You may not always have the flexibility you do right now, so take advantage of it and pull everything you can out of this precious season in your life! When you look back, you will see this time as a gift.

I want to take the rest of this chapter to give you some insights into what kind of baggage you may be carrying and equip you with helpful tools. Because digging deep can sometimes feel heavy, I've created a list that brings specific clarification to different patterns of baggage and brokenness that God wants us to overcome. As you read through, be prayerful and allow the Holy Spirit to shine a light on these areas. Remember, the goal is not to see how many issues we have, but to continue to submit our lives to the Lord so He can form us into all we are meant to be. We are all works in progress, and this process of singleness can be a beautiful time to let Him make you healthy and whole.

Every one of us has things we need to work through. I believe self-awareness is key to our personal development. Being aware of our triggers and how things affect us is essential in walking out our personal freedom and wholeness. Below are some key behavior patterns I have observed through the years that I believe are symptoms of deep-rooted issues in people's lives.

Pattern #1: Always in a Relationship

This person doesn't know how to be single. In many ways they don't know how to live as a single person because they've consistently been in a relationship the majority of their life. They go from relationship to relationship, and as one relationship ends, they already have another one beginning. They don't know what it's like to be their own person, single, happy, and thriving. Being single feels scary to them, and even though they have felt the Lord ask them to be so for a season, they don't know how.

I think there are specific times God may ask us to be single for a reason. Maybe He wants to extract or add something to us that will help us become healthy, whole, and more like Him. Jumping from relationship to relationship is like a person on an operating table who won't be still. They won't allow the surgeon to do the work. They never stay on God's operating table of "singleness" long enough to allow God to do what He needs to do in order to prepare them for their future. When we don't take the time to allow God to encounter us and work His truth and love into us, we never benefit from the opportunity of learning from our past mistakes and failed relationships. In order to be whole people who are solid in our identity in Christ, we must take the time to learn from our past and allow God to do some work in us. Taking the time to be single and deal with our stuff is essential for us to mature and grow in God. Rebounding into the next relationship only creates a facade of forward movement, and what we don't realize is we are leaving parts of who we are behind. We have to take the time to get to know ourselves outside of a relationship and develop who we are in the Lord as an individual before we step into marriage. When people get out of a relationship, they often want to jump into another simply to stop missing their ex and not feel the loss and disappointment of that failed relationship. But another relationship isn't going to heal you. Only Jesus is.

Remember when God told Abraham that he was going to have a biological son? Because of how long they waited and how they viewed their limitations, Abraham and his wife produced a son through Sarah's maidservant. That is how his son Ishmael came to be. This story is a picture of what happens when we try to make something happen in our own timing. We create things that are counterfeit versions of what God wants to give us. When we don't trust God in our singleness, we go from relationship to relationship trying to make a certain person our "God match." It would be like if Abraham started going from maidservant to maidservant trying to create a new Ishmael, all with the intent to force God's promise to come to pass. But God's intention was not to bring His promise about through a maidservant but through Abraham's wife, and for it to be Isaac, not Ishmael. When we wait on God to lead us, He will give us His best, not a counterfeit version of what we have been praying for. We have to let go of what is not working to grab a hold of what God wants to bring into our life. People who bounce around are looking for someone to meet a need that only God can. It's time to quit playing the Ex Games. If marriage is something the Lord has for you, then you can't be distracted by past obsessions.

Pattern #2: Long-Term Friendships Falling Out

This is a person who has a consistent pattern of long-term friendships imploding. Typically this happens when someone has unresolved issues that make it difficult for them to have honest and vulnerable long-term friendships. Fear of intimacy eliminates the ability to have healthy and authentic relationships with people. People will only be vulnerable with you if they think you are being vulnerable with them. If you aren't willing to go there, over time, the relationship will become stagnant and shallow. Because of this cycle of implosion, people like this tend to have a new best friend every few years. It is not normal for people to go through best friends like we go through pairs of jeans. Each of us should have long-term, healthy relationships that last through the years. Authenticity, vulnerability, honor, respect, confidentiality, trust, loyalty, etc. are all characteristics we practice in long-term friendships. These are also fundamental components for building healthy marriages. If we have created a pattern in our lives where our close friendships fall apart every couple of years, what will happen when we get married? We will be at risk of carrying that same pattern into marriage.

Pattern #3: Drama Is Your Normal

Listen. None of us needs more drama in our lives. If you are interested in someone who has drama as their default button, I have one word for you: *Run!* One thing I have learned in pastoring people for years is that drama attracts drama! When someone has habitual patterns of crazy and chaos in their life, it is pretty safe to say there are some deep-rooted issues that need to be addressed. But understand that it's equally dysfunctional if you are someone who is consistently choosing relationships with people who have a lot of drama and chaos. If you are intentionally allowing their toxic behavior into your life, that is a sign that there is something dysfunctional in you. A healthy person does not choose a toxic person. The people we allow to come into our lives are a mirror of what is going on inside us. This cycle of dysfunction has to be eradicated in us. In order for a marriage to thrive and grow, drama cannot be the normal.

Pattern #4: Doesn't Respond Well to Constructive Feedback

If someone you have a relationship with can never challenge your decisions, attitude, lifestyle, etc. then that's a problem.

The people we are close to should have the ability to speak into our lives. When people challenge you and your immediate response is to cut them out of your life, that is an issue. We need people in our lives who will challenge us. Listening to what they have to say and being willing to make changes is a key part of growing and maturing! For a relationship to be healthy, it requires healthy communication and feedback. If you cannot receive feedback and be humble enough to look at yourself honestly, it will be hard for you to have a happy marriage. A spouse needs to know they can approach their loved one about anything. There shouldn't be topics that are off limits. There may be things that are sensitive, difficult, and even awkward to talk about, but a healthy relationship can handle the weight of awkward and sensitive conversations. Someone who is open to honest feedback is much more likely to have a marriage that lasts, is happy, and thrives!

These are just a few ways for us to take some honest inventory of ourselves and see if there are things in our lives that need to be addressed. None of us will ever be perfect, please know that. But I do think we need to be intentional about addressing issues in our lives. We need to move towards being whole people, especially if marriage is something we desire. Coming into this covenant relationship healthy and whole sets our marriage up to be a place of joy and fulfillment. When we bring all of our unresolved dysfunction into marriage, not only can it sabotage the potential for a great marriage, it can also weaken the foundation we are building our future on.

Our foundation gets built when we put the right things in place under our feet. When you think about that necessary layer, we don't have to go any further than the Bible. The Word talks about building our lives on God the Rock:

> *Therefore everyone who hears these words of mine and puts them into practice is like a wise man who built his house on the rock. The rain came down, the streams rose, and the winds blew and beat against that house; yet it did not fall, because it had its foundation on the rock. But everyone who hears these words of mine and does not put them into practice is like a foolish man who built his house on sand. The rain came down, the streams rose, and the winds blew and beat against that house, and it fell with a great crash.* (Matthew 7:24-27 NIV)

Allowing God to come into our lives, set our identities on Him, and heal the foundation of our belief system is building our foundation on the Rock. The issues and behaviors in our lives that are not dealt with are the sand that causes us to falter and fall when the storms of life rage. Everything gets destroyed because what we have built our lives on isn't stable or secure. The only true stability and security you can have in life is anchoring yourself in Jesus.

Healthy Vulnerability

Vulnerability is a bit of a trendy word. It's cool to have the appearance of "being honest" and "true to yourself," but that's not always healthy or appropriate. There is a big difference between healthy vulnerability and telling the world your darkest secrets. Many times, we think being vulnerable is sharing every little tidbit of our lives on social media or spouting off about what is annoying us at that moment. That's not real vulnerability—that's actually more like vomit. We need to operate with *healthy* vulnerability. It is not about you and I updating our social media status or tweeting our current mood. Pause with me for a moment and understand that I love you enough to say this: Social media is not your diary. Repeat after me: *"Social media is not my diary."* Seriously. That is just a counterfeit version of vulnerability. Let's look at some other things that can hinder healthy vulnerability.

1. Disappointment with people, so you learn to stop expecting anything.
2. Because of past disappointment, you always question someone's motives if they are being nice to you.
3. When good things happen, you find yourself waiting for something bad to happen.
4. People open up to you, but you don't open up to others.
5. You have zero margin for error in relationships, and because we are obviously all imperfect people, you leave a trail of sabotaged relationships.

6. If someone does something you view as "not treating you right," you end the relationship.

I believe that after Jesus takes us through the process of healing in our lives, it is those places of former brokenness that can become our greatest places of authority! God can take us from our distrusting, suspicious, critical, judgmental, controlling old selves and turn us into people who look and love like Him. But we have to be willing to give Him our stuff! The Lord wants to dig out the roots of whatever is keeping us from being who He created us to be!

We all long to be fully known. For that to happen, we must be vulnerable. The only way we can experience authenticity in relationships is by taking off the masks we wear and allowing ourselves to be fully seen by God. He, of course, always sees beyond the masks we wear, but when we take them off ourselves and choose to show ourselves to God, that is when a real, deep relationship begins to take place. When we feel fully known by God, then we know what is to be fully loved by God.

Creating Space in Your Emotional Real Estate

When we get healthy, we are removing the destructive and self-sabotaging behaviors in our lives. This creates space in our emotional real estate. Emotionally, each of us only has a certain capacity. Some people have larger emotional capacities, and for others it's very small. Typically, the smaller the emotional capacity you have, the more baggage and issues you are consistently fighting through. Negative emotions and traits can take up a lot of emotional space in your life without you fully knowing it.

Anger, unforgiveness, and bitterness shut down love, peace, joy, compassion, and empathy—all things we need in our lives to walk in healthy and whole relationships. When you go through the process of pursuing emotional wholeness and well-being, you will be amazed at how much more you feel you can handle. All of us will experience negative emotions, of course, but when we are fighting through emotional junk in our lives, it affects even our ability to problem-solve and cope with the challenges of everyday life.

I know when I am struggling with a person or a situation, and then I get bad news or something else goes wrong, I can quickly hit my emotional capacity. Why? Because negativity takes up so much more emotional space than positivity. We can never have too many positive emotions! Isn't it interesting that when you are in a place of peace and joy, even if you get bad news or have to deal with an unexpected difficult situation, it is easier to keep perspective and your peace through it?

This is why it is so important to regularly assess your emotional state and the condition of your heart. Are you depressed, which is often connected to unresolved issues or latent anger? Are you losing your temper quickly and can't seem to control emotional outbursts? Are you critical and quick to find things wrong in both people and situations? Being in a season of singleness is the perfect time to deal with the destructive and self-sabotaging behaviors in our lives. You might think, *I only lose my temper once in a while.* Well, I want to lovingly challenge your thinking. We are called to walk in the fruits of the Spirit every day of our lives. We shouldn't be losing our tempers and having outbursts of anger or rage. Some of you may want to argue that Jesus "lost his temper" when He went into the temple and flipped tables because they had defiled the house of God. Well, that was a righteous, holy anger and, let's be honest, when we lose our temper or have emotional outbursts, it is rarely because of a righteous and holy anger. If we do not deal with our stuff, our stuff will deal with us. Unresolved issues will rob us from the fullness of what God has for us.

Galatians 5 talks about what types of fruit we should have in our lives as followers of Jesus:

> *But the Holy Spirit produces this kind of fruit in our lives: Love, joy, peace, patience, kindness, goodness, faithfulness, gentleness, and self-control. There is no law against these things!* (Galatians 5:22-23 NLT)

If you do not have these fruits in your life, then Jesus isn't done bringing healing and wholeness to you. As sons and daughters of God, the fruit of the Spirit should be our norm. There needs to be evidence of His Spirit dwelling and moving through us. If we look at our lives and see that the fruits of the Spirit are not flowing consistently, then it is a wonderful time to take inventory of any false beliefs in our lives. When the lies of the enemy are exposed, that is when God breaks through and sets us free. Recognizing and owning the places where we need God to heal and deliver us is an invitation for transformation!

On a practical level, here are some examples of traits that can damage and destroy relationships as well as limit the fruit of the Spirit in our lives. This list is certainly not exhaustive, but these are common practical ways in which bondage from the enemy can play out in our lives. I want to encourage you to not read this section for someone else but read it for yourself. When God begins to challenge us, it's always easy to think of someone we believe needs to hear this, but maybe God is speaking to *you*. Maybe this moment is actually a setup from the Lord for your freedom. Too many of us live a life of only partial freedom and deliverance when full freedom is available!

Examples of troublesome traits:

1. **Lack of Confidentiality:** People who are not able to keep sensitive information to themselves and feel compelled to share it with other people, even when they have been asked not to—especially when that information could hurt others.

2. **Lying:** Because of fear or issues of self-worth, people who lie are often trying to protect themselves. They may feel like the truth isn't interesting enough or it doesn't help support the image they are trying to create.

3. **Gossip:** People who love to be "in the know" and have information about other people they shouldn't have. They love being the person who is the first to expose this information by sharing it with other

people, especially when it is at the expense of someone else.

4. **Critical Nature:** These people are quick to point out or notice all the flaws in other people and situations. Those who have a critical nature often feel the need to share their observations with others.

5. **Road Rage:** When another driver does something they view as unsafe or unfair, they feel the need to "tell" that person and impose their feelings on the drivers around them. At times, this can turn verbal and physical.

6. **Fits of Anger:** This person typically raises their voice, says hurtful things, and negatively affects the environment they are in. People do not feel safe with them.

7. **Control:** These people have a difficult time working with others and with delegating things. They feel they have to do everything themselves for it to be done right. They want people and things to be a certain way and close relationships often implode from being controlled.

8. **Suspicious:** This person questions people's motives and intentions and has a hard time trusting.

9. **Victim Spirit:** This person expects things to go wrong for them and regularly rehearses past struggles and traumas inwardly or verbally with others. They build relationships based around their trauma and issues.

10. **Pride:** These people exhibit ego, arrogance, and elitism, often believing they are better and more deserving than other people.

11. **Being Unteachable:** These people have little-to-no accountability and will not allow people to speak into their lives.

12. **Easily Offended:** These people take everything personally and are overly sensitive.

13. **Insecurity:** These people struggle with self-worth and comparison. They never feel good enough.

14. **Moodiness:** These people's moods change quickly and often. If things don't go their way, their mood is instantly affected. This changes atmospheres negatively.

15. **Performance Mentality:** These people constantly try to prove their value to themselves, others, and God. They will often strive for someone else's acceptance, even to the detriment of their own well-being.

If you struggle with any of these things, God wants to set you free! As I stated before, He did not die on the cross so you could live in partial freedom! He died on the cross so you could live in full, abundant freedom! We are called to be people who walk in the Spirit, but we live in a society that has given permission for the flesh to run wild. It's becoming acceptable to post every ungodly emotion on social media and say whatever fleshly accusation or opinion you have, as long as you preface it with, "I'm just being honest." Friends, I want to call us higher—I want to call us into our full identity in Christ Jesus.

There are so many reasons why we do what we do. Most of the time, dysfunctional behaviors and distorted belief systems are either learned behaviors or coping mechanisms that are created throughout our lives. Sometimes we are so determined not to repeat the sins of our family line or our past that we live a life full of striving and perfectionism. But to walk in freedom, we need to allow Jesus to get to the root, so these things are demolished once and for all. Jesus didn't call us to live a life of striving, He called us to live a life of freedom.

Re-Identifying Your Personality

When something has been a part of our personality for a long time, it's easy for us to think it's "just the way we are," when, in fact, it's a learned behavior, not the sanctified version of who God created you and me to be. This is the process I call "breaking free from false identification." A good example of this is when someone knows they have a temper, but since most people in their family have a temper, it feels normal to them. But you and I both know that shouldn't be someone's normal. Just because it's normal in your family doesn't mean it's healthy behavior. It simply means that the trait of anger you deal with is a learned behavior from the environment you were born into.

What if I told you that each of us was created with a specific personality, and those personalities have a sanctified and unsanctified version to them? Here are some examples:

1. Justice vs. Vengeance
2. Mercy vs. Co-Dependence

3. Leader vs. Dictator
4. Excellence vs. Perfectionism
5. Unwavering vs. Stubborn or Rigid
6. Pure vs. Legalistic or Self-Righteous
7. Administrative vs. Bossy
8. Introvert vs. Aloof
9. Extrovert vs. Overbearing

You may be thinking, *But I am so much better than I used to be! You should have seen my life before I came to Jesus!* As true as that may be, and please know I am celebrating every bit of breakthrough with you, I believe if we do not see the fruit of God's Spirit daily in our lives, then more healing, breakthrough, and transformation are available to us! Don't allow partial breakthrough to be your stopping point in the transformation process Jesus has for you. When you and I were born again, we were grafted into a new family line where every generational curse and bondage of the enemy can be broken. There is good news for you! The struggles of your mom, dad, grandparents, and siblings do not need to be *your* struggles. Jesus can write a new story in your life—one that will be a living example of His transforming power!

Stop Comparing

Another mindset that can limit our freedom is when we look at those around us and think we are good just because we believe we are doing better than they are! Just because you are doing better than those around you doesn't necessarily mean you are walking in full freedom. Honestly, it depends on whom you've surrounded yourself with. Are they living fully for God and walking in their own personal freedom? If the answer is no, then my challenge to you is to not let the brokenness of those around you be the barometer by which you measure your personal freedom. If you are going to honestly evaluate where you are emotionally, spiritually, and mentally, then make sure your gauge is lined up with His Word and His Spirit.

On the other side, you may compare yourself so much to others that you never feel good enough. You live from such an intense level of comparison to those around you that, by your standards, you're always coming up short. You become so hard on yourself and you never really celebrate the fact that you are created in the image of God your Father. For you, this season is to learn to see yourself as He sees you!

Be Who You Would Want to Marry

Be the type of person you actually want to marry. When I was pastoring, and especially when I was directing schools of ministry, I had so many young men come into my office and say, "I want a girl who is super hot, loves working out, and is super fit." I would look at these guys and think, *Well son, then you better be that person you want to marry. 24-Hour Fitness is down the road. It's $29.95 a month.* I'm just saying. Don't demand something from someone else you're not willing to give.

It's amazing how many standards we have for other people that we don't apply to ourselves. We want someone super generous, but then we are stingy. We want someone who is kind, patient, and gracious, but then we are judgmental and critical. All those traits you are praying and believing for should be happening in your life first. Then, see what you attract. It's about living healthy, whole, and empowered because you're actually owning your life and owning your behavior. When we do this, we are going to have healthy relationships in our lives because we are operating from the truest version of who we are created to be.

If marriage is something the Lord has for you, imagine what a different place you will be making that decision from when you allow Him to bring complete freedom to your life! When we go after personal freedom and inner healing, it positively affects everything. It impacts the people we surround ourselves with, the decisions we make, the way we see ourselves, what we believe for, and how we dream. It also determines the type of person we choose to marry and most definitely influences our marriage and home life. Getting healed, healthy, and whole is so key to you experiencing God's highest for you. Because when you get free, your generations get free!

You Aren't Waiting To Be Chosen, You Choose

I remember growing up there were some unspoken rules in society when it came to finding a spouse, and one of them, specifically for women, was if you were pretty enough, thin enough, and sweet enough, then men would pursue you. If you were too full-figured, too loud, too sassy, too this or too that, then your likelihood of being pursued diminished significantly. Let's establish right here and right now, you are enough and you are not too much.

As women, we were taught to be what a man would find attractive in hopes of enticing pursuers. Growing up, someone's physical appearance was 90% of why we had a crush on them. It wasn't until you matured that you realized physical appearance is only an aspect of the equation. So many of us women were groomed to sit pretty in hopes to catch some man's attention and, ultimately, get married, if we didn't do something to mess it up.

This is unhealthy thinking and not at all the posture I believe we are called to have. We are not perfect. I am not perfect, you are not perfect, and anyone married will tell you their spouse is not perfect. So, why do we feel led to hide who we really are during our attempt to entice or get someone's attention? If we simply lived authentic to who we are, how much more fulfilling would our relationships be!

To all the singles, you do not have to wear the right outfit, say the right thing, display the perfect balance of being available, but not too available, or be at the right weight or have your makeup just perfect, or be whatever else you feel is required for you to get yourself into a relationship.

There is so much pressure to be everything we believe someone is looking for that we forget one key truth. You are not waiting to be chosen, but you have the opportunity to choose. In all our effort to be noticed or catch the attention of a possible suitor, we forget our own role throughout this process. You choose whether or not they are someone you want to be with. Do they meet your standards? You choose whether you open up your life to them. Remember, you are not waiting only to settle for the enemy's counterfeit.

Just because someone pursues you does not mean you have any obligation to be in a relationship with that person, even if you haven't been in a relationship for years. I know during my nineteen years of being single, different men would pursue me, yet I knew they were not who the Lord had for me. My nonexistent love life did not obligate me to go on dates I didn't want to go on, nor be in relationships with men I had no desire to date. You have a voice in your process. The Lord is always our guide and He will lead you just as He did me. I waited on Him and His peace, but I also believe the Lord invites us to be part of our story. We are not robots simply obeying orders. We are in a love relationship with the Lord, and He wants you to be present and participating in your story!

ZERO IN ON:

➤ **Negative emotions and traits can take up a lot of emotional space in your life without you fully knowing it.**

➤ **The only way we can experience authenticity in relationships is by taking off the masks we wear and allowing ourselves to be fully seen by God.**

➤ All those traits you are praying and believing for should be happening in your life first. Then, see what you attract.

➤ Don't let your relationship status dictate the life you are meant to live now.

➤ You aren't waiting to be chosen, you choose.

09

REMOVING THE PAUSE BUTTON FROM YOUR LIFE

When you're waiting to meet someone special, it's so easy to unknowingly push the pause button in certain areas of your life. When you're single and ready to mingle, it's easy to gravitate toward the mindset, "When I get married, then I will _____." Fill in the blank and you find out where you have put your life on pause. It's easy to do this, because naturally, we all have preconceived timelines as to how we think our life is supposed to unfold. So we wait. We wait to buy the first house. We wait to make that move to the new city or take the new job. We wait to try new hobbies and make major life decisions. Why? Because, quietly, we want those moments to be shared with our spouse, and those major life changes and milestones are connected to marriage for us. Many of us quietly believe home ownership only happens with marriage, which, of course, isn't true. But because that may be more "normal" and "typical," we create these rules we were never supposed to live by.

I want to encourage you to *live your life* and remove the pause button from it! Take risks, buy that home, take that new job, move to the new city, and check off some of those boxes on your bucket list of life! Stop waiting and start living!

When I was in my early thirties, I had the opportunity to buy a condo, my first big purchase. I always thought I was going to make that purchase with my husband. I had mixed emotions about doing this alone, but I also knew I would be missing out on opportunities in life if I waited for something I didn't have control over. I didn't know when or if the Lord would bring my husband, but I knew He had plans for my life—plans that were supposed to be lived out *now*. So, I had to make the choice to move forward with what the Lord was placing in my path and stop waiting.

Just to encourage you, I've lived overseas, moved to different states, traveled to various nations, bought a condo, accepted new jobs, and pastored—all while being single. Early on, I made the intentional choice to live my life fully and not put things on hold waiting for marriage. Would I have preferred to do all of these things with my husband? Sure, but I'm so glad I didn't wait because all of those experiences made me who I am. I took risks, embraced the unknown, and met the most incredible people along the way. I have memories and life experiences I wouldn't trade, and I wouldn't have had any of those if I had chosen to wait and see if I got married first. Had I done that, I would have waited a very long time. Think about how much of my life I would have wasted. Instead, I followed God through the open doors and lived my life fully. That is so much more fulfilling than the alternative!

Pursuing the Call

One of the best decisions I ever made as a single person was to pursue the call of God on my life no matter my relationship status. I knew I was called to preach, prophesy, and pastor. Many times, I encountered the stigma of being a single woman in ministry, and each time I had to step over that ignorant thinking and know that God commissioned *all* women to preach and minister, not just the married ones!

Matthew 28:18-20 records the Great Commission Jesus gave to His disciples:

> *Jesus came and told his disciples, "I have been given all authority in heaven and on earth. Therefore, go and make disciples of all the nations, baptizing them in the name of the Father and the Son and the Holy Spirit. Teach these new disciples to obey all the commands I have given you. And be sure of this: I am with you always, even to the end of the age." (Matthew 28:18-20 NLT)*

This is a mandate to *every* believer, both men and women. We are *all* called to walk in the authority of heaven here on earth and to go make disciples of the nations, baptizing them and teaching them the gospel of Jesus Christ. This is our mandate as sons and daughters of God and has nothing to do with our marital status! You are not exempt because you are single or in a waiting season. All of us are called to share the good news of Jesus Christ through our lives and words, whatever form that takes.

As a single woman in a ministry position, I faced various challenges. The local radio station in the town where I was an associate pastor played weekly sermons of the pastors in the city, but they refused to play my teachings because I was a woman. In that same town, I also had people come to the church for a Sunday service when I was preaching, only to learn after the fact that they had staged a silent protest. These people were in agreement that if the senior pastor allowed an unmarried woman to preach, then they would get up and leave. This happened several times. I also had the local newspaper decide not to print any of my sermons in the newspaper, something they did for the pastors in the area, because I was an unmarried female. This was just some of the pushback I endured, but I refused to let it deter me or allow it to create excuses in me that limited who God called me to be! I share the above challenges to let you know it's not always easy or convenient to trust God in your single season. But if you are committed to pursuing the call of God on your life, then it is worth it! Don't ever apologize for living out who God created you to be!

As a single woman pursuing the call of God on my life, I was greatly impacted by generals of the faith who paved the way for us today! I read about Kathryn Kuhlman, Smith Wigglesworth, Maria Woodworth-Etter, Aimee Semple-McPherson, John G. Lake, and William Seymour, just to name a few. I read the stories of these great men and women of God and learned about the persecution and challenges they all faced, which were much more severe than anything I had ever experienced. Their stories marked me with a resolve that no matter what ignorant thinking or obstacle I hit, I would keep going hard after God. So what if a newspaper and a radio station wouldn't release my teachings? I wasn't going to let that stop me from preaching the gospel. And so what if people protested as I preached, walking out and disrupting the service? My life was created to give God glory and that's exactly what I intended to do. I chose to turn whatever challenges I faced into something positive. I recognized that I wouldn't be getting resistance if I wasn't making an impact.

I hope through these stories you are encouraged to not lessen your pursuit and love for Jesus! As a single person, it's easy in our society to think that we have to "chill out" a little bit, not get so "radical" for Jesus, or not be all "holy" for God. The enemy can very quietly and subtly whisper lies to us, convincing us that if we go too hard after God, no one will want to marry us, and we will be forced to be single for the rest of our lives. I've been saying this throughout my life, and I will continue to say it. I don't know if you're going to get married, but I *do* know that if you have to dull down your love and pursuit of Jesus for someone to pursue you, then you have the wrong people in pursuit! My attitude was that I am a strong and fiery preacher and if that was too much for a man, then he was not the right man for me! I had many people through the years tell me that I intimidated men and my response was, "If I intimidate them, then they aren't strong enough for me!" I truly believe we should never have to dull our shine, quench our fire, or quiet our voice to be more appealing for someone. You want someone to value you and cherish you for who you are, not who you are pretending to be. You and I are called to be carriers of the gospel—to heal the sick, cast out demons, and set the captives free! Don't wait any longer—start living that calling out now!

> *Heal the sick, cleanse the lepers, raise the dead,*
> *cast out demons. Freely you have received,*
> *freely give.* (Matthew 10:8 NKJV)

Our calling is not just determined by our skill level or obvious talents. It is something that was spoken over us and put within us way before we were worried about our relationship status. We don't have any excuse when it comes to the plans God has for our lives. A verse that speaks to this (one of my life verses) is:

"Before I formed you in the womb, I knew you;
Before you were born, I sanctified you;
I ordained you a prophet to the nations."
Then said I:
"Ah, Lord God!
Behold, I cannot speak, for I am a youth."
But the Lord said to me:
"Do not say, 'I am a youth,'
For you shall go to all to whom I send you,
And whatever I command you, you shall speak.
Do not be afraid of their faces,
For I am with you to deliver you," says the Lord.
Then the Lord put forth His hand and touched my
mouth, and the Lord said to me:
"Behold, I have put My words in your mouth.
See, I have this day set you over the nations and over the
kingdoms,
To root out and to pull down,
To destroy and to throw down,
To build and to plant." (Jeremiah 1:5-10 NKJV)

I love this because Jeremiah is so relatable. As God is telling him who he is and prophesying his purpose and destiny, Jeremiah reveals a lie he has believed, which has become an excuse for him not to live out his destiny. Jeremiah says, "But I can't speak, for I am a youth." He felt like his age disqualified him and that he had nothing to say. That may not be your excuse, but what is? What have you allowed to hold you back? Imagine God saying to you everything He is saying to Jeremiah. What begins to rise up in you that would argue against this powerful destiny? Those are the lies that have become truth in your life. These manifest as excuses and have created the pause buttons in your life. It may be your singleness, age, or financial situation. Whatever your excuse is, I need you to know that's really all it is. Removing the excuses in our lives removes the pause button. When we stop giving reasons why we aren't living in the fullness of who the Lord declared us to be, we then stop allowing the excuses to limit us or make us miss out on living out our dreams!

What I love about Jeremiah is that he allowed God to win this argument. God touched Jeremiah's mouth. When He did this, Jeremiah allowed God to remove his excuse. It was in that moment that Jeremiah became one of the greatest prophets of the Old Testament. But this couldn't have happened until an exchange took place. God had to destroy the lie and replace it with the truth.

God wants to make the same exchange in your life, so that the lies of the enemy that have held you back are destroyed and the truths that will release you into your destiny and call take root. Because I'm focusing on the journey of singleness and you living fulfilled in it, let me address that area. I want to say to you that you do not need to be married to be good enough. You are already good enough. You do not need to be married to be called of God. You are already called of God. You do not need to be married to be qualified. You are already qualified.

Every lie and every word curse that has been spoken by someone else or by yourself, let the Lord break that off and replace it with His truth. Consider what we discussed in the previous chapter and understand that you don't have to live under any lie. You are called, qualified, anointed, and powerful regardless of your marital status. Marriage was always created to be a complement to your life. It was never created to complete you. Only God can do that.

When the Lord brings two people together for His purposes, it is such an exciting thing! But I believe living your life fully for God before marriage is essential to creating both the depth and personal relationship you need. Many people fall into the mindset that when they get married or have kids, they will then start going to church regularly and reading the Word more consistently. But we all know the habits you create before you get into a marriage are what's going to form the foundation as well as the culture of that marriage.

If you want a marriage and a home built around the Lord, then your life needs to be that. Yes, you will build upon what you both bring into a marriage together, but that stems from what you are currently building as a single person. For marriage, I believe it is essential that you know who you are in the Lord as an individual. My husband can't build my relationship with Jesus. That is something I have to do on my own. He can't pray my prayers for me or read the Word for me. I have to do that if I want to go deeper in my relationship with Jesus. Just like I can't worship Jesus for my husband—he has to do that himself. We can encourage one another in our walks with the Lord and we can pray and worship together, but that doesn't replace what Jesus and I cultivate on our own! If you are not spending time with Jesus as a single person, then what makes you think you are going to spend time with Him once you get married? It doesn't work that way. No matter how great a spouse you may have one day, that person can't always be your comforter, your refuge, your source of joy and peace. That can only truly come from Jesus. If that is not solidified in your personal walk with the Lord, then that it is something you will quickly learn you need in marriage. Jesus must be your source and foundation.

Living Full of Hope

The Lord spoke to me in specific ways when my heart needed to be encouraged the most during my years of waiting. He is always so faithful to bring a needed word at the right time! Proverbs 16:24 couldn't be truer!

> *Nothing is more appealing than speaking beautiful, life-giving words. For they release sweetness to our souls and inner healing to our spirits.* (Proverbs 16:24 TPT)

It was in the moments where hope seemed to be the far-thest away that God, in His constant faithfulness, would always show me His heart for me and the circumstances I was facing. God doesn't let you stay in the valley. He walks you through the valley of the shadow of death and brings you to a place of rest and peace.

It was in one of those moments when the Lord was dialoguing with me about marriage that He said something that changed my perspective concerning my expectation of what marriage was to be. Somewhere along the line, I had picked up a belief that when I got married, I would be complete. That day the Lord whispered to my heart, "You're always complete in Me. Marriage will be a complement to what I am already doing in you." This dramatically shifted my thinking and expectation! I wasn't waiting to be completed—I was already complete in Christ! I was already a whole person, fully loving and living my life. If the Lord was going to bring someone into my life, then He would bring someone who would complement what He was already doing.

That mindset shift really affected the decisions I made. I tore up the mental list of things I was waiting to experience or do if I got married, and began to fully live my life and stop waiting on the unknowns. Marriage is not the answer to all the problems and challenges you are facing. Jesus is the answer. The more you lean into Jesus and deepen your walk with Him, the more content and at peace you will be!

Live each day knowing who you are and who God has called you to be! You have been given access to His entire kingdom! Everywhere you go, you carry Him with you. There will always be people who will try and hold you back, limit your thinking, and diminish how you see yourself. Let me be at least one voice in your life who reminds you of who you are created to be. Don't let yourself be boxed in. Allow God to write His story through you, which will include some adventures and you taking risks! In this season of your life, He is extending His hand to you, encouraging you to let go of the pause button and step out of your comfort zone. As you do this, you will start experiencing the thrill of completely giving all you are to Jesus. Every day, you have the opportunity to choose which voice you listen to. We can listen to the lies of the enemy telling us we need to wait until we are married to fully pursue God, and that we can only make a major life change once we are married. Or you can listen to the voice of God asking, "Will you trust Me?" It's time you start fully living and allow God to take away the option of the pause button once and for all.

The greatest honor and privilege you and I have is to give our lives to the Lord. By removing all conditions and pause buttons in our relationship with Jesus, we create a life based on Him, which is the only thing that guarantees true peace and happiness. Removing the pause buttons off our dreams and lives is incredibly freeing and exciting! If marriage is something the Lord has for you, you'll have plenty of firsts and new experiences in marriage. Don't put your life on hold for something that is unknown. Start living now without limitations on everything the Lord wants to do in you and through you!

ZERO IN ON:

➤ Never dull your shine, quench your fire, or quiet your voice to be more appealing for someone. You want someone to value you and cherish you for who you are, not who you are pretending to be.

➤ Marriage was always created to be a complement to your life. It was never created to complete you. Only God can do that.

➤ Start living now without limitations on everything the Lord wants to do in you and through you!

10

CREATING AN ON-RAMP FOR PURSUIT

For so many of my single years, I felt veiled by the Lord. It was as though there was a divine covering placed over me. Years would go by with very little pursuit by men, and then there would be seasons where multiple men pursued me at the same time. The majority of my nineteen years being single, I found myself relatively unnoticed by men. It was as though guys looked right over me, like they just didn't notice me in the room. It didn't necessarily feel personal or like punishment. I could feel the divine nature of the situation. I knew the Lord had shielded me because of the purposes He had for me.

I know this might sound strange, so let me try to explain. I always had a lot of male friendships in my life and was very comfortable around men. But the majority of the time they didn't seem to look at me in a romantic way. This made me feel kept and hidden by the Lord. I could feel His protection and jealousy over me. This veiling was God's doing, not man's. But although I knew this was the Lord, there were times it was so difficult to be content while being veiled. There were times I was so tired of waiting and I just wanted God to do it already. But one thing I learned was that, regardless of feast or famine in the area of pursuit, I had to wait on the Lord to say "Yes" because I knew none of the men pursuing me during those nineteen years were who the Lord had for me.

When I hit age thirty-eight, it felt like all of sudden I was actually being seen by men! I knew in the Spirit that something had shifted, but I definitely experienced a shift in the natural too! It seemed clear that marriage was on the heart of God for me. It felt like any single man within a hundred-mile radius was in full pursuit. It was strange, surreal, and honestly overwhelming. I knew God was up to something. I was in a place in my life I had never been before. So I began to seek the Lord on how to walk this whole thing out. The Lord led me through some very practical steps that I believe can help you as you navigate this for yourself.

Creating Emotional Space for Someone Else

So you're ready for a relationship! Great! Many people say they are ready, but they don't make adjustments in their life to create space for a relationship. That's right, space. There has to be room in your life for a relationship because relationships take time, priority, and effort. Many of our lives are so full that, even if someone came along whom we could see a future with, where would they fit? So many of us are overscheduled already, so to add anything else and think it's going to thrive is not realistic. We have to create space in our lives for relationships.

Remember what I shared in Chapter 8? If all of your emotional space is taken up, where is someone else going to fit? When you are healthy and whole, you are able to clear out the debris from the storms of trauma that had you maxed out all those years before. The key is not to stay stuck in your stuff. If you constantly have to work on your own personal freedom without breakthrough happening at some point, then there isn't typically space for another person. I've encountered so many people who are *always* working through past pain and/or trauma. Don't get me wrong, I love it when someone is being proactive about getting healthy and healed. But there also has to come a point where you *are healed* and moving forward. There has to be a day when you are no longer fighting for your freedom, but you *are free*!

I am not trying to rush someone's process or shame someone for taking longer than usual. Please hear me. If you have heard anything throughout these pages, it's that I value the uniqueness of our journeys. I am simply trying to say that there comes a point as a son and daughter of God when you are healed, healthy, and whole. None of us will ever be perfect, and that isn't the goal. However, there does come a point when past issues in our lives have been resolved and we are moving forward emotionally, mentally, and spiritually free!

I know this is not easy, but for the sake of our friendships and relationships, this is so essential. Until you deal with the issues in your life head-on, you will be dealing with the same patterns and cycles you have been in for years. Having a healthy, thriving relationship in your life when you haven't dealt with your issues will be, at minimum, difficult. If you take your un-dealt-with stuff into marriage, it's as though you are stunting its growth before you've even started. Jesus doesn't want you to have a hard marriage. He wants you to have a marriage where you are able to be fully loved and receive someone else's love. He wants your marriage to be free from anger issues, suspicion, self-centeredness, and resentment. The first years of marriage don't have to be so hard if we deal with our stuff while we are single.

Here's also another thing to think about. When we are bound up in our own issues, our focus often becomes on ourselves. What many people fail to realize is, when we have things in our lives we haven't dealt with, the people around us often become our "counselors." I think it's good to be transparent and open with the people you are in close relationship with, but there should also be boundaries with this. If you are constantly needing to "process" and have people rescue you from your spirals, then you should consider going to counseling. Godly counseling, when done right, can be a great outlet for someone to gain their freedom without overwhelming those around them.

When you are getting to know someone and believe there may be potential for a long-term relationship, be absolutely honest with who you are and where you are in life. But also recognize that when you are getting to know someone, that is not the time for an inner healing session. Get your inner healing and your pastoral needs met outside of your dates. Creating emotional space for another person is key. In order to do that, we have to be able to get out of ourselves and be emotionally available for someone else.

Be Accessible: Learn How to Engage with What's Around You

Another thing I learned was not only to be available but also *accessible*. That means get off your phone, look up, and engage in the world around you. Doing life with people is more than interacting via social media and texting. It's talking, laughing, and connecting. Being in the physical presence of someone has so much more richness than a digital connection. When someone talks to you, respond back with more than a one-word answer. Be friendly, warm, and engaging in conversations. Make yourself emotionally and relationally accessible. If you get asked out to coffee, ask the Lord if you have permission to go, and if He says "Yes," then go and enjoy. Don't make the person wait two weeks to get coffee with you because you're so busy. That goes back to my first point. You have to create space to be pursued and, ultimately, space for a relationship. If you don't have accessibility in your life, potential prospects will see that and will often be discouraged from pursuing you.

Now, don't go crazy on me and stop everything. Live your life fully, but create an on-ramp for accessibility for someone to join you in that full life.

We have to create space in our lives where someone actually has the opportunity to get to know us. People feel the vibes you're giving off. If you are single in your status, but not accessible to get to know, you've just voided out a lot of great people who could be amazing gifts in your life. I think sometimes we get so busy and focused on the goals and tasks at hand that we can become inaccessible to people who would love to get to know us. I'm not just referring to romantic relationships here, I am talking about friendships as well. If we are always rushing around, stressed, busy, and maxed out, then we will feel too busy to hang out with people. Be aware of the vibe you are sending out to the people around you. Accessibility creates on-ramps for relationships. Making space in our emotional capacity means making space with our time. We have to create space in our lives for the people we love to connect and build on-going relationships with us.

I don't live in the same city as some of my closest girlfriends, so we have to be intentional about making time to connect. When our schedules are crazy, we plan calls with each other, grab a cup of coffee, and talk for two hours. We also schedule a few days each year to take a trip together to get some face-to-face time with each other. We all have a lot going on and time feels like it is moving faster than ever, but those are covenant relationships in my life. I want to take time for them. We all take time for what is a priority in our lives. So, if being in a relationship is a priority for you, then creating space and time is essential.

Lastly, when we are getting to know people we could potentially see ourselves dating, as Christians, we can make this really weird. There is this strange pressure to *know* if that is our spouse or not on our first date. For most people, this isn't realistic and is something that takes time to discover. But, because of this obsession with getting married, so many single Christians use the first date as an interrogation to see if the other person meets their criteria. I would encourage you to stop trying to figure out if someone is your spouse and just get to know them as a person. You're not saying, "I do." You're just having a cup of coffee.

Thoughts on Dating

The word "dating" is oftentimes viewed like a cuss word in the Christian world. Obviously, there needs to be both wisdom and boundaries when it comes to dating. But dating is simply two people getting to know each other. It takes time to get to know someone. So again, it's not always realistic for us to think that we can "know" right away if a person is someone we could see a future with.

When I use the word "dating," I am referring simply to getting to know someone the *Lord has given you permission to get to know* and that is *not sexual*. A mature definition of healthy dating can be defined like this:

DATING: When two mature, healthy, God-fearing adults take time to get to know one another.

Because people are people and they distort what should be a natural thing, dating has become this interview session, filled with pass/fail questions and sexual tension. People. That is not dating. That is Match.com. To the person who thinks the Lord has given them permission to date anyone and everyone within the church, can I lovingly encourage you to go back and recalibrate your ear to hear God? I encourage you to take a break from your version of dating and allow the Lord to heal whatever it is that you are trying to fill.

I did go on a handful of dates throughout the nineteen years. But those were few and far between. Whenever I felt the peace of the Lord to get to know someone, I always invited Holy Spirit to lead me through the process. And then I waited on the Lord to know if I was to go on another date. By keeping Jesus at the center, it keeps our ears and our hearts connected to His. Before Sean, each time I heard a clear "No" from the Lord, I didn't allow anything else to develop. Keeping your heart surrendered to the Lord during this process is critical because God is so good at protecting us and always ensuring we get His best!

Something strange and surprising I encountered during those years were the men telling me God had told them I was their wife. This happened at least a half-dozen times. I had no relationship with these men when they told me this, and barely knew any of them. But they were convinced of what they heard, so I had to gently let them know God had not told me that, and I was not interested.

I share this with you because I do believe God does speak to us, *but* I don't believe we always have to share what we feel like we are hearing. That certainly applies to this scenario. If you feel like the Lord has highlighted someone to you, and you can see marriage in your future with them, then keep that to yourself. If you heard correctly, then the Lord will bring it to pass naturally. If it wasn't God, then it will be a good learning lesson for you moving forward. When we want something so badly, it is easy to believe we hear certain things. I don't want anyone to become insecure in their ability to hear God. But I do want us to exercise caution when it comes to matters of the heart. Be encouraged with this. When it is God, you don't have to make it happen—He does that! When we share things like this, it can put a lot of unnecessary pressure on the natural process of getting to know someone. I would encourage you to keep these things between you and the Lord and pray into them. He has to be the One to do it anyway!

I would also encourage you not to try and figure it out all at once. I think we need to bring back the healthy scenarios of single people being able to get to know each other in an organic and natural way. We need to remove the pressure of people having to know if someone is the "one" immediately. Additionally, when we keep the physical out of the process of getting to know someone, it keeps things simple and clear. And look, I'm only talking about kissing and holding hands at this point, nothing more, but even this can quickly become unnecessarily complicated and confusing!

Every person's journey is different. Some people know right away if someone is a match for them. But the majority of people don't. Here is my point: Use wisdom and discretion, and guard each other's hearts. Above all else, listen to the leading of the Lord. If you do not have peace, then don't let anything develop. Listening to the warnings and guidance of the Lord will keep you in a place of peace. That is what we all want.

God calls us to handle people's hearts with care! We have to be intentional with how we steward someone's emotions, keeping in mind how we would want our heart to be treated. When someone has given us their heart, whether we feel the same about them or not, how we interact with them is so important. Their interest in us can be flattering and make us feel good. We can get so caught up in how good it feels that we forget we are dealing with a real person's heart and get sloppy with how we treat them. We can easily find ourselves leading them on because we are focusing on our needs getting met, not realizing we are being careless with them. Not only is this unhealthy, it's detrimental to the people involved. If you are distracted by only getting your needs met, you may miss out on someone who could be a great fit for you. When people observe us not handling other people's hearts with care, they often won't be interested in having a relationship with us. How we walk out this part of our story has a huge impact on our reputation. Understand that people see how we treat others. We must walk in wisdom and integrity on all levels when it comes to pursuing someone.

Think Outside the Box

Be willing to hang out with new people! Ask people to hang out whom you are interested in getting to know but haven't had a chance to. Go and try new places and do new things! Be open and willing to encounter different people in different ways. This is such a great way to open yourself up to something new.

The Lord really challenged me to think outside the box as He was preparing to bring Sean into my life. If you know me personally, then that wouldn't be something you would think was hard for me. I naturally think outside the box on most things, except for when it came to the type of guy I was going to marry (if God was going to do that in my life). I had such a predictable picture of what my husband might be like. But when God brought Sean into my life, he came in a very different package than what I expected. He and I had totally different upbringings and life experiences. He was older than me and of another race. Sean and I are different in so many ways and the packages we both bring to our marriage differ from what we expected. But it's been so good, and it's been so God! Honestly, it's our differences that have made us stronger and what I have come to love and appreciate! All of our life experiences make us who we are, and I can honestly say our marriage is better for it. I love that we serve a God who isn't predictable. He does things in ways that always surprise us. But when we are willing to live outside the box and color outside the lines, what a fun adventure God will take us on!

I can truly say that as I have surrendered my preferences to God, I have experienced the greatest joy and blessings in my life. I love how much Sean has taught me about his race, culture, and all the wisdom he has gained through his life experiences. I am a better person for all of this. And that goes both ways. Sean is better because of what I bring into his life. The Lord knew we needed each other and gave us both such a gift by bringing us together. But, if I had not been open to God breaking down my box, then I may have missed the greatest gift God has ever given me.

Sometimes we can feel like we are settling if we go outside the lines or step outside the box. We can feel like we are lowering our standards when we do something different than what we expected. Believe me, I'm all about standards—hence the reason I was single for nineteen years. But I don't think it's compromising to be open to God taking you out of your comfort zone. I've never felt like I settled by stepping outside the box of how I pictured my marriage relationship. If anything, when I married Sean, I felt like I got a serious upgrade in my life! I've never been loved the way Sean loves me, and what a gift to have a husband who daily puts Christ at the center of our home. Different doesn't equal settling. Different is just different, and sometimes different is exactly what you need!

You have to be willing to live outside the lines. You have to be willing to be stretched or challenged in your mindset. When we open ourselves up to God, we have to know there is a good chance He is going to do things differently than what we expected. Your spouse may come in a different package, and it might be the best thing you never knew you needed!

Tearing Up the List

I don't know who started it, but in the Christian community creating a "list" of everything you are believing for in a spouse is a very popular practice. The list includes their love for Jesus and other wonderful traits, which hey, I don't have a problem with. But then people take it too far and start picking eye color, hair color, the profession the spouse should be in, their financial status, and what type of car they should drive. At that point I've got to say, *Stop!* I'm all about having faith and I believe in the power of declarations, but when your list gets that specific, it feels like you've moved beyond declarations and are now standing in the land of manipulation.

It's not wrong to have preferences and/or a type, but you and I know it doesn't always turn out like that. This isn't Starbucks where you can get your coffee just the way you like it. This is about saying, "Jesus, I am open and available for who *You* have for me, whatever that looks like." Think about how many married people you know who have shared that their spouse didn't come in the package they thought. Yet, they couldn't be happier. That person is the best fit for them.

Pray for your spouse to have the traits found in Galatians 5. Pray for them to love Jesus with their whole heart and love you like Jesus loves you. That is a great way to pray. My prayer was always, "Jesus, let me marry a man who is running so hard after You I can barely keep up!" Well, He answered my prayer. My husband *loves Jesus!* He is always going after more of God. I love it and it provokes me to do the same. I have a husband who loves the Word and is a man of prayer, surrendered to the Lord in every part of His life. What a gift I have been given!

> *Do not be unequally yoked with unbe-*
> *lievers. For what partnership has righ-*
> *teousness with lawlessness? Or what*
> *fellowship has light with darkness?*
> (2 Corinthians 6:14 ESV)

You want to have a home that is centered on Jesus. Jesus is the foundation for what you build your family and marriage upon. That is the most important thing. For those of you who have made a list for your future spouse, can I encourage you to look it over once again? Are the non-negotiables on your list really that important?

Pray and declare the things that matter! Pray for a patient spouse who is kind and loving. You want a person who is humble and knows how to honor the Lord and you. It is these things that matter, not what kind of car they drive and the clothes they wear. Granted, I get it, we all want there to be chemistry. Absolutely! If you are going to have sex with your spouse for the rest of your life, you better have some chemistry! But chemistry isn't the foundation of your marriage. Neither is it that person's swag or style. As much as that might matter to you, be open to whom the Lord may have for you.

What were my non-negotiables? I knew my future spouse and I had to have the same value system, had to love Jesus full-on, and not live a compartmentalized Christianity. He had to be generous and kind, and I knew my husband had to have a sense of humor because laughing is one of my favorite things. And if I was ordering my spouse at the drive-through of heaven I would also add, "I'll take a 6'1", African-American, super-hot, and fully ripped man!" Oh wait, I got that! LOL!

Now hear me. I am not saying the Lord is going to bring you some lame, completely boring person and because they love Jesus you should just make it work. Of course not! But I am saying you should allow the Lord to tear up the part of your list that is not really important. Be open, because a lot of great people come in really different packages! You may think you have a "type," but the *best* person for you might not be your typical "type." I tell people to tear up their list, not because I'm against being specific in your desires, but because many times people's lists are actually "wish lists" and not lists of things that really matter.

As I just shared, I wanted a man who was surrendered to Jesus and had a great sense of humor. I wanted laughter to be a constant in our home. I wanted a man who was generous and kind and with whom I had great chemistry. That's it. I kept it simple intentionally because I knew those things were my non-negotiables. There was no way I was going to be with someone I couldn't laugh with. Laughter is huge for me. Generosity and kindness are two of my favorite traits of Jesus, and because I value those traits so much, I knew I wanted them in my husband. And of course, I wanted a man who ran hard after Jesus. I wasn't driven by a list that demanded my husband be in full-time ministry. Honestly, that didn't matter to me. What mattered to me was his relationship with Jesus, not if he was ever on a platform or not.

Guess what? I got all those things and so much more! I have a husband who exhibits the fruits of the Spirit daily and is fully surrendered to the things of the Lord. I also have a husband who has incredible style and swag for days! Our chemistry is off the charts and that's because God knew exactly what I needed and then threw in some extra! Because that is Jesus! We even have the privilege of traveling across the world to various nations ministering together. Trust Jesus to know what you need. Sean was different than what I expected in so many ways and I love all the surprises he came with.

Ripping up your list doesn't mean letting go of your non-negotiables, but choosing a spouse is not an ordering system. You can pray into things and, again, have your non-negotiables determined, but make the list short and leave the rest to God. Have realistic expectations. Let the Lord know the important traits you think you need, then surrender it. You have to trust God to make the match. You have to trust God to bring the right hearts together. I want to encourage you to be open to what God may do. Maybe it will look exactly as you saw it happening, but maybe it won't. Tear up that long, over-detailed list that is restricting things the Lord may want to do! We serve an out-of-the-box kind of God!

Relationships Require Risk

If you're uncomfortable with risk, then you probably shouldn't be in a relationship. Healthy, growing relationships require risk. It takes risk to be vulnerable, honest, held accountable, and fully known by someone else. There are no guarantees in a relationship. You're opening yourself to another person, running the risk of getting hurt and stepping into the unknown. But you have to be willing to take risks and put yourself out there, because what you can get in return, when God does it, is one of the greatest gifts—love.

If you are really going to be open to a relationship, then you have to be committed to the process of vulnerability. If we do get married, we all want a great marriage! But a great marriage takes effort, intentionality, and yes, risk. We have to step up and have the hard conversations sometimes and ask for the things we need. Great marriages don't have secrets or masks. They have honesty and trust. If you are not healthy and whole, this will feel impossible. But, if Jesus has healed you and set you free, then this is absolutely possible when He is at the center.

When we give our heart to someone, we don't have control over how they will handle it. We have to trust them, and we have to trust the Lord with them. Solid, thriving relationships go beyond the surface and require a deep dive into vulnerability. The greatest marriages are where people are accepted and loved for who they are, not for who they will become. But that is only possible if you have first learned to love and accept yourself.

Trying to Make it Happen

When feelings of desperation kick in, it's hard to trust God! That's when so many of us are tempted to take matters into our own hands. I want to challenge the modern-day dating culture and let you in on a little secret. When you are living for Jesus and trusting Him with your desire for marriage, that takes the pressure off you! When I felt the clock of my life ticking away, I just wanted to make it happen, but I always felt the Lord encouraging me to trust His timing. He would say, "Christa, relax, I've got you!" Meaning, He is taking care of me and I don't have to worry! That is true for you too! When you have given Him your dreams and desires, be confident that He will work everything out! He will always take care of you. Why? Because He loves you! You are His kid and it's safe to say you are His favorite! He wants what is best for you and He knows the desires of your heart.

Don't Stop Being You

Okay. I'm not trying to brag, but I do a legit goat imperson-ation! I didn't come up with it, so I can't take credit for creat-ing it. But during a late-night study group in college, this guy showed us his goat call. It was so ugly and hilarious. I loved it! We all gave it a try and from that point on—I owned it! When I do the goat call, I distort my face and it's super ugly, but so funny it's worth it.

Right after I learned it, I came home for the holidays and, being the little sister of course, I showed my family the goat call. They all died laughing! I then went on to teach all my nieces and nephew the goat call as well. It became an instant hit! My sisters used to joke, "When you meet your husband, don't show him your goat call!" We would all laugh really hard and I would always respond, "That is the first thing I am going to show him, because if he likes me after that, we are good to go!"

Of course, I am not saying you should be gross or ugly—I am saying just be yourself. You might be quirky or have unique tastes, but be honest about who you are. You want to have relationships (not just romantic, but friendships too) where people like you for you. It's a much less exhausting way to live your life.

For women, we so often feel like we have to look super cute, be really thin, and have our hair and makeup on point, but it's not true! When Sean pursued me, it wasn't because I was in the right place at the right time, looking the right way, or saying the right thing. It was because it was the Lord's timing and the Lord unveiled us to one another. For the first time, I really "saw" Sean. Sean and I knew each other as ministry acquaintances for years. I was on staff at a church where he was a regular guest speaker. I was the director of a school of ministry, and whenever he spoke on Sundays, we asked him to stay over to teach at the school on Monday. He was always my students' favorite and someone I greatly respected. But it wasn't until years later that we actually saw each other in a new way. It's always amazing to me that when God gives the green light to a situation, it is then you will see people and situations differently.

I enjoy getting ready, wearing an outfit I love, and doing my hair and makeup like a lot of women. I'll always do that. But I also know there is not a pressure, nor should there be, to look and act a certain way to keep the attention of my husband. He loves me. In the same way, if you have to look a certain way or act a certain way to keep the attention of someone while you are dating, then it's probably not someone you want to build a future with. I feel equally loved when I am all made up and when I first wake up in the morning. You want the kind of love that goes deeper than the surface.

Give Them Something to Work With

One thing I have never believed in is playing games with people's hearts. I am very much a straight shooter and what you see is what you get. I like everyone until they give me a reason not to, and even then, I ask Jesus to give me a heart for them because He still loves them. I've always been upfront about what I think and feel, so I take this approach into the relationships in my life, whether it be in my family or with friends or my church community. I've always tried to be someone who is open to relationships and lovingly honest.

As you know, before Sean, I was never in a serious relationship and I didn't have a lot of dating experience. Because of that, I was not versed in playing games or even playing hard to get. When Sean started pursuing me, I took the approach to be true to my heart and not make the process hard on him or unnecessarily difficult. I saw so many people playing hard to get and thinking it was cool not to appear "too excited" about the person. The problem with that is they always seemed underwhelmed. If I was the pursuer, that would definitely deter me. I think anyone who is putting his or her heart out there needs something to work with.

With Sean, I let him lead the pursuit, but I always responded to his pursuit. He took a step out on the plank of risk with his heart and I matched his step. He shared his love for me, and I shared mine right back. I never made it hard to know what I was thinking or feeling, and I think that is important. I think the healthiest relationships are ones that are candid and honest. No topic is off limits and hearts are vulnerable. That is what makes us feel safe and known. If I can trust you with my heart, then I can trust you completely.

I think it's time we put away childish games and immature mindsets. If you want a mature, healthy relationship in your life, then mind games don't have a place. No one wants to play anymore. What people want is relationships with people they know are true to who they say they are. You are an adult and you owe it to yourself to have a mature and authentic relationship.

Is There Only One for Me?

I often get asked about whether or not I believe in the "one." Because so many people come from various walks of life, I come at it from this angle. I do think there is God's best for each person, but I don't know if I would say there is only one person for every individual. If I believed there was only one person, then what about the widow or the one who went through a divorce they never wanted? Are they never to have hope again for a fulfilling, God-centered marriage? Of course not. I believe the Lord can bring people into all the different chapters in our lives, even the places we didn't expect to find ourselves in.

I want to encourage your heart today. Perhaps you are single and not by choice. Maybe your spouse had an affair, or bondage with addiction destroyed the marriage you once had. Maybe you found yourself a widow unexpectedly and you are just now entertaining the idea of possibly opening up your heart again. Or maybe you got married to someone before you were walking with the Lord, and now you're divorced and want a marriage very different from your last experience. Then of course, perhaps you have never been married and you've been on the journey of learning what it is to be content in your singleness yet contending for the desire of marriage in your life!

Whatever the reason you are single, I want you to know there is *hope*. Jesus is never done writing your story. I truly believe if your story isn't good yet, then God isn't done writing it! One of my favorite portions of Scripture is Psalm 139. I love it because it shows how deeply and intimately the Lord knows *you*. With an estimated seven billion people on planet earth, I love that our God still knows every detail about you and me. You are not just one of many—you are the one who has captured His heart and attention!

Let's be reminded by looking at Psalm 139 in its entirety:

O LORD, you have examined my heart
and know everything about me.
You know when I sit down or stand up.
You know my thoughts even when I'm far away.
You see me when I travel
and when I rest at home.
You know everything I do.
You know what I am going to say
even before I say it, LORD.
You go before me and follow me.
You place your hand of blessing on my head.
Such knowledge is too wonderful for me,
too great for me to understand!
I can never escape from your Spirit!
I can never get away from your presence!
If I go up to heaven, you are there;

if I go down to the grave, you are there.

If I ride the wings of the morning,

if I dwell by the farthest oceans,

even there your hand will guide me,

and your strength will support me.

I could ask the darkness to hide me

and the light around me to become night—

but even in darkness I cannot hide from you.

To you the night shines as bright as day.

Darkness and light are the same to you.

You made all the delicate, inner parts of my body

and knit me together in my mother's womb.

Thank you for making me so wonderfully complex!

Your workmanship is marvelous—how well I know it.

You watched me as I was being formed in utter seclusion,

as I was woven together in the dark of the womb.

You saw me before I was born.

Every day of my life was recorded in your book.

Every moment was laid out before a single day had passed.

How precious are your thoughts about me, O God.

They cannot be numbered!

I can't even count them; they outnumber the grains of sand!

And when I wake up, you are still with me!

O God, if only you would destroy the wicked!

Get out of my life, you murderers!

They blaspheme you; your enemies misuse your name.

O LORD, shouldn't I hate those who hate you?

Shouldn't I despise those who oppose you?
Yes, I hate them with total hatred,
for your enemies are my enemies.
Search me, O God, and know my heart;
test me and know my anxious thoughts.
Point out anything in me that offends you,
and lead me along the path of everlasting life.
(Psalm 139 NLT)

Every single word of Psalm 139 brings comfort to me! It should bring so much hope and peace to your soul (your mind, will, and emotions). Because it is God's written Word, we can't argue with His love for us! He knows when you sit down, and He knows when you stand up. He is with you when you are going, and He is with you when you are coming. He knows everything about you! He has blessed every part of your life. You cannot hide from His presence because He is always pursuing you. He will find you in the darkness and bring you back to the light. You cannot escape Him! He knew you when you were merely substance and He was there forming you in your mother's womb with destiny in His heart over your life. Your name is written on His heart. He is constantly thinking about you. You cannot comprehend His love for you. He is with you always, will never leave you, and is always going before you and covering every step you take.

I meditate regularly on Psalm 139 because it always brings everything into perspective. Remember the quote from my husband that I shared earlier: Ninety percent of warfare is per-spective. How true it is! The enemy is all about distorting your perspective on who God is and who you are. When you need a perspective shift, meditate on this: He's got you and He's not finished writing your story!

The wonderful thing about the Lord is He prepares you for the chapters of your life. If there is a day when the Lord brings someone into your life and you experience the journey of being pursued, allow Him to lead that process. What I shared in this chapter is merely what the Lord showed me and took me through, but know you will have your own journey and process. As you continue to trust God with the dreams and desires of your heart, rest in the fact that if He opens up the door to marriage, He will also guide you through that journey.

ZERO IN ON:

➤ We have to create space in our lives for relationships.

➤ Get your inner healing and pastoral needs met outside of your dates.

➤ If you are single in your status, but not accessible, you've just voided out what could be your life's most amazing gift.

➤ You are an adult and you owe it to yourself to have a mature and authentic relationship.

11
PURITY VS. VIRGINITY

When it comes to purity, I think so many of us have been looking at this the wrong way. The common question I get when people find out I got married at thirty-nine is, "Were you a virgin?" I always find it odd that people are so fixated on whether someone is a virgin or not when they get married, because honestly, I think there are many people who get married who are technically "virgins" but didn't walk in purity. For me, purity goes deeper than not having sex before marriage.

Listen, if you are still fixated on the question of if I was a virgin or not, the answer is yes. Yes, I was a thirty-nine-and-three-quarters-year-old virgin when I got married. Sounds like a movie doesn't it? But the reason I was able to be a thirty-nine-and-three-quarters-year-old virgin was because my motive wasn't to be a virgin, my motive was to walk in *purity*.

We all know people (no fingers being pointed, I promise) who did "everything" *but* have sex because their motive was to be able to technically answer "yes" to being a virgin if asked. But, honestly, if you have to get technical about your virginity, then you've missed the whole point. We are called to walk in holiness and righteousness. That takes virginity to a whole other level. If we are going to walk in purity, then that means we need to guard ourselves from situations and people who would encourage us to cross lines we know violate what we've committed to the Lord.

A great place to start when trying to understand what purity looks like is to practically evaluate what you are allowing into your life to entertain you—the TV shows you watch, the movies you go to, the music you listen to. What is the focus of those things? If there is a lot of sexual content, nudity, and suggestive images, all of that goes into the mind and memory bank. We can pull all of those images and pictures up at any given time. We are foolish to think we can watch or listen to sexually explicit movies and music and believe it won't affect us. Not only is that not true, but I believe it affects us much more than we really know. Have you ever watched a rom-com movie and then found yourself suddenly bummed out that you are not in a relationship—especially when you were previously in a great mood? You suddenly feel sad, weepy, emotional, and maybe even angry about your singleness.

What you watch and/or listen to *does* affect you. It's like when you watch a show that has explicit sex scenes and then wonder why you are suddenly thinking about making that booty call you had previously been delivered from. You reason that because you're not the one technically doing the things you're watching, then it's fine. It's innocent, right? No, it's actually not, because it stirs up within you desires and appetites that don't need to be awakened, and it affects you spiritually, physically, emotionally, and mentally. Every part of us is impacted by what we watch and listen to. Watching and/or listening to sexually focused things is not going to help you walk in purity and will do nothing but sabotage you.

This isn't as popular as it used to be, but I remember growing up with so many women who were into those graphic romantic novels (hello, *Fifty Shades of Grey!*) and many Christian women I knew were reading these books and thinking it was fun and might spice up their sex life. The only thing this will actually do is give you a distorted view of what a healthy sex life is supposed to look like. Your sex life isn't about control, manipulation, or domination. Sex was always created to represent covenant.

When you are dating, you are practicing covenant—not in the sexual sense but in the relational sense. Some may say that you are not in covenant with the person you are dating because you are not married yet. Well, that is true and not true. Look at it like this. When you are dating someone, you expect that person to be faithful to you, to not be with other people, whether that be sexually or emotionally. You have a healthy expectation that they will be loyal to you and committed to you and *only* you. If that person makes the decision to step outside the relationship and hook up with someone else or become emotionally attached to another person, you would naturally feel betrayed and cheated on. We can all agree that is true. I call your expectation and practice of faithfulness and commitment to one another as practicing covenant. You are making a choice to honor that person, respect that person, be faithful to that person, and not give yourself to another. That is covenant, and although you are not married, you are still living out what that looks like in preparation for marriage if the relationship comes to that.

What is crazy is that some people cannot be committed or faithful to one person while they are dating, and they think that will change when they get married. If you haven't been able to be faithful in practicing covenant while dating, then what makes you think you will be able to live out covenant when you're married? It is not a switch that is flipped once you say, "I do." Covenant is a lifestyle. It's a set of convictions and core values and is a daily surrendered choice. Just like your relationship with God, you choose to live a life that honors Him. You have a "free will" to make whatever choices you like, but because you are in covenant with Jesus, there is a clear set of beliefs by which you have chosen to live your life. That is covenant. Covenant isn't forced, it's chosen. In any relationship, friendship, dating, or marriage, covenant is a daily choice. It is choosing to honor and love that person, sometimes above your personal preferences, and it is about honoring the Lord every day.

The same goes for purity in a dating relationship. You are living out what covenant looks like to the other person.

Covenant looks like respect and honor, not pressing or crossing boundaries. It's about guarding one another from situations or things that would cause them to cross a line.

So, what does this look like practically? Here are some things I have learned in walking out this journey:

1. Know your convictions and make sure they line up with the Word of God.

2. When in a relationship, have a conversation where you both agree on the boundaries. That way you are not trying to figure it out in the heat of the moment, because we all know that does not work. Hormones speak louder than logic in those moments.

3. Make sure you are both on the same page. By having agreed-upon boundaries and convictions, it's not up to one person to always be the boundary enforcer for the relationship. It should be two mature, godly people having an equally yoked relationship to ensure it is built on the foundation you have both committed to.

4. Set a limit on how much time the two of you spend by yourselves. It is really easy to cross boundaries when you are always alone with someone. Go out, do things together, be with other people, and enjoy the community you are building together.

5. Nothing good happens after midnight. I'm kidding, but not kidding. For some of you, it may be 10:00 p.m. For others 8:00 p.m. Whatever time your guard comes down is the time when you should avoid being

alone together. Recognize that when we are tired, we don't always make the best decisions. So, set yourselves up for success and have set times when people need to go home.

6. Be accountable to others. We all need people in our lives to whom we are accountable. They are people who will remind us of our convictions and morals if we ever find ourselves wavering. These people are the ones you go to when you are struggling and hopefully before any compromise is happening. These are the ones you are totally honest and transparent with so they can truly come alongside you. Your accountability partner is not someone who is "figuring it out" with you. No, this needs to be someone who is mature in their walk with the Lord. They aren't someone who will just tell you what you want to hear, but will tell you the truth. We all need people in our lives who will call us higher. They are also people who will remind you of who you are and often be able to see things that may be a blind spot to you.

7. Use wisdom in your communication. What you say, text, and communicate has a huge impact on the purity of a relationship. It's very common for people to text each other sexually suggestive things with the intent to flirt or keep it spicy and exciting. But what they may not understand is that type of conversation before marriage only stokes a fire that isn't supposed to be burning yet. Be careful of what you

arouse. You can still keep it spicy and exciting without it being sexually arousing. This helps not only guard one another but also honors the convictions and boundaries you have agreed to.

Again, walking in purity is so much more than just being a virgin. It's about honoring God. I heard someone say this once and I loved it. When facing situations where we are trying to make decisions concerning areas of purity, a good question to ask yourself is, "Does this make me feel *clean*? Does it honor God and the instructions of His Word? Would my conscience be clear if I did this?"

Those questions are a much better gauge for you as you walk out purity then simply saying, "We aren't going to have sex." Well, is sex just intercourse or does it include oral? Even the medical world would say oral sex is sex, but many people somehow don't believe it is. My motive here isn't to bring condemnation or shame—quite the opposite. Instead, I want you to re-evaluate how you look at sexual intimacy. We all want intimacy, but we want it to be a healthy, Christ-centered intimacy that comes with emotional connectedness first with God, then with one another.

Intimacy is taking off your mask and showing others who you really are. It is the next level after vulnerability. Intimacy is communication and listening to one another. That is actually much harder than taking off your clothes. Intimacy is being honest about why you don't want to disrobe and why it is so important to you to honor God in all aspects of your relationship. This type of vulnerability is about being authentic to who

God created you to be. In a world full of so much pressure to conform, this can be much harder than we realize, especially when you care about someone and your heart is involved.

What is sad is that there was a time when "Christians" had the same convictions and standards when it came to dating and walking in purity. But in today's society, this is not something that can be assumed. There are many people who identify as Christians and yet, their standards and convictions are very different from one another. Don't make the assumption that just because you met them at church or Bible college that you two are on the same page. Always recognize you are your own person and you are empowered to set and enforce the boundaries and convictions you feel led to live by. Don't allow another person's lack of conviction and compromise to dull your standards. Know who you are.

I wasn't a thirty-nine-year-old virgin by accident. I was a thirty-nine-year-old virgin because I made many choices to guard my purity. Even as a young teenage girl, I quickly realized if I wanted to walk in purity, I could not live by the standards of those around me. My resolve for purity came through personal encounters between the Lord and me. Those convictions weren't forced on me by other people or persuaded by culture. They were created by spending time in God's presence and in His Word. What is the Lord speaking to *you*? As you study His Word and listen to Holy Spirit, allow Him to speak to this area of your life. When you know who you are in Him, it is a lot easier to align yourself with people who bring you closer to God and don't pull you away from Him. When you are rooted and grounded in Him, it becomes much easier to discern who really has your best interest in mind. You will have the discernment to know who is really living for the Lord or who is simply telling you what you want to hear because they want to get with you.

I know choosing a lifestyle of purity may be new for you. It can be scary to put yourself in a position where the person you care about may walk out because you were honest about your morals and convictions. But I want to encourage you that if they leave you because you are choosing to walk in purity, then that is a good indicator they are not the right person for you anyway. If they don't share the same core values and convictions with you, it will be very difficult for you to have a healthy, drama-free relationship with them—let alone marriage. Trust me, you do not want an unequally yoked marriage. Keep in mind, this is a person you will build family with, possibly raise children with, and share finances with. You need to have the same core values and convictions—your destiny is too important to settle for anything less than God's best!

ZERO IN ON:

➤ **Your sex life isn't about control, manipulation, or domination. Sex was always created to represent covenant.**

➤ **Covenant looks like respect and honor, not pressing or crossing boundaries.**

➤ **Don't allow another person's lack of conviction and compromise to dull your standards. Know who you are.**

12

YOU ARE A CARRIER OF THIS MESSAGE

You are a trusted carrier of the message of singleness! You may not have wanted it, but here you are! Now the question is, what are you going to do with what you have been given?

Years ago, I had to make a mental decision that I would not be a single woman who was bitter, desperate, or living a small life because I never got married. I wanted to show the generation coming behind me, watching me, that even if I never got married, I was going to be happy, thriving, and fulfilled! That was not some facade I was creating. It was a result of everything I had walked through and the journey of singleness the Lord had marked me with! I really had to come to a place where I was happy, thriving, and excited about my life. I wasn't just faking it to make it—I believed it. And I still do! Many times

I've had young people tell me that they loved how I was pastoring, preaching, and going fully for God while happy and content in my singleness. I shared with them that it took time for me to get to that place, but that it was absolutely possible to be unmarried and live a totally fulfilled life.

As I grew up, I remember meeting people who never got married. They seemed unhappy, sad, and some even seemed bitter. They made being single look miserable and unappealing. I didn't want to repeat that cycle. I wanted to show my nieces and nephew, as well as the people I was pastoring, that marriage doesn't equal happiness, nor does it determine whether or not I live out the call of God on my life. Being a trusted carrier of this message is bigger than just me and you! It's for the people around us. It's for the people who don't know Jesus yet, and who are going through relationship after relationship because they are in search of something only Jesus can provide. You and I can show them they don't have to keep going from one-night stand to another to feel some sort of intimacy and connection. They can come to Jesus and He will encounter them with a love they didn't even know was available!

I believe that as we refuse to lower our convictions and pursuit of Jesus, it will help spur on those around us. For those of us who have the privilege of walking daily with Jesus, my hope is that our lives display the joy and fulfillment of putting Him first. And for the people who don't know the Lord, my prayer is that they see our lives as displays of the goodness and faithfulness of God! I want people to look at our lives and see that we will love and serve Jesus regardless of whether or not our prayers and desires get answered. Let us be people who are always pointing others back to Jesus no matter where we find ourselves in life. None of what we do is in our own strength, but it is always found in His strength. We have the incredible opportunity to live one life for God. Don't waste it worrying over the things we have no control over! The gift of singleness is a message that the masses need. Marriage is not your goal, Jesus is.

Letting God Write Your Story

As you can tell, this is not just another book for me. This is something I have lived. It is something I put nineteen years of my life into, and even though I'm in an incredible marriage now, the journey continues on. I'll always be surrendering, learning to trust deeper, and waiting for prayers to get answered. The process isn't over, and it actually never ends, but that's the beauty of Jesus. He's always inviting us deeper, to trust Him more.

I married a man who had been married before. I love our story. I waited till I was thirty-nine years old to get married, but my husband had been previously married and had a whole other life before me. He went through a divorce, and although he walked through it circumspectly, he still faced many unknowns concerning his future. While he was going through that painful time, the Lord was taking me through the journey of laying marriage on the altar and giving Him all of who I was. At the end of that journey, I thought I was never going to get married.

Then the Lord shocked us both and reconnected us. Only the Lord could have written our story and brought us together. We hadn't seen each other in three years and had completely lost touch when God ordained our paths to cross once again. Although Sean and I walked different journeys, we couldn't be more perfect for each other. Our love runs deep, and when I reflect on the story of how God orchestrated our relationship, I know that only He could have written it.

Some of you may relate to Sean's experience. He was divorced and uncertain of his future. He was heartbroken and running to God to heal his heart. It was in the embrace of the Lord where Sean's heart was healed and restored. And then there came a day when he began to dream about the future. If you are walking through loss and heartbreaking situations, there is so much hope for you! Allow the Lord to heal you and restore the parts that have been beaten up and broken. God is so good at restoring everything that has been lost. He is the God of restoration and second chances. It's when we are downtrodden and broken that the enemy wants to come in like a flood and taunt us, telling us it's over, that we're finished. But God raises His standard so that the enemy's taunts are silenced once and for all. In those moments, God covers us with His grace and love. Take your pain and disappointment to Jesus. As He heals your heart, He will also redeem your story. The goal isn't to get married again—the goal is to walk intimately with the Lord all the days of your life. As you allow Him to undo every violation of the enemy, you will see His covenant reinforced!

Maybe you relate more to my story and you've been single for what feels like forever. For the most part, I was the exception, not the rule. But I know there are many who can relate with the long wait. The desire for marriage has been laid down, but not forgotten. You long for it, but hope feels far away. I want you to know that God can do anything at any time. In one moment, He can take nineteen years of waiting and change everything. He is the God of suddenlies, and even though the years have passed, and the window may feel closed, it's never completely shut when God is writing the story. I've waited so many years for so many breakthroughs and promises to come to pass in my life. Honestly, most blessings I have received have taken years to be fulfilled. I have been forced to learn patience. I've learned that even though the timelines I created weren't fulfilled, God fulfilled them in His timing. When the focus of your life is loving Him versus all your dreams being fulfilled, you are able to wait on Him and His timing. When God brought Sean into my life, I wasn't expecting it and yet I was open because I was living in the delicate tension of being content in my singleness, yet believing that if this was of the Lord, He would do it.

Offering Vs. Sacrifice

People often ask me how I found a place of peace and contentment as I walked out so many years of singleness. When I was first asked this question, I had to take time to evaluate my journey because, honestly, I wasn't sure how I got there.

Then one day, I realized what the *key* was. It was when I shifted from seeing my surrender as a *sacrifice* to being an *offering* to the Lord. Both are still choices, but one feels painful and one feels joyful. My sacrifice and surrender initially felt painful, but in time, my trust and love for the Lord deepened and I began to find joy in my sacrifice. When joy entered my perspective, everything shifted for me. Because I had joy in my sacrifice, it then became an offering I chose and gladly gave to the Lord! I remember so many times I would be overcome with His goodness and kindness over me that I would find myself shouting to the Lord, with tears streaming down my face, "You can have all of me! I'm all Yours! I hold nothing back, take it all! I give it freely, I give it willingly! Because You are so worthy, Jesus, let my life be a joyful offering before You!" When that became my cry, the pain, the sacrifice, and every price I had paid was no longer my focus. I found true joy in my offering.

Even now, I still pull on that revelation of the joyful offering for current places of surrender in my life. Again and again, we will be asked to lay things down before the Lord, but *how* we lay them down is just as important as *what* we lay down. The Lord loves a cheerful giver (2 Cor. 9:7). What a difference it makes on our internal state when we don't begrudgingly surrender, but are joyfully surrendered! When we live from the place where we choose to lay an offering on the altar of the Lord, there is a joy that comes simply from being able to worship and give to Jesus, our Savior. He gave His life for me and for you! What a joy to be able to give to Him!

I believe I was able to get to this place of a "joyful offering" by spending time with the Lord and allowing Him to access my heart fully. When our heart fully trusts, fully relies on, and fully loves Jesus, then it is so much easier to give things away and lay things down. When we fully trust Who we are giving it to, then we can be confident that no matter the outcome, He loves us and cares for us. He will work *all* things out for His glory, which makes everything we have walked through worth it! Let everything be for His glory!

Whatever your reason for being single, divorced, or widowed, God has you! If marriage is something the Lord has in store for you, then He will make it clear. But regardless of the desire for marriage, use this time of being single to lean closer into Jesus, joyfully offer all that you are to Him, and let Him do what only He can do—heal you, restore you, and set you free! Jesus created you for relationship with Him, and what a gift we have been given. Don't squander the gift of singleness and the precious time you've been given. As Paul said, this is the time you are able to give your undivided attention to Jesus. Take advantage of it!

Remember, if Jesus brings that significant someone into your life, everything you sowed during your single years will be reaped in your married years. All the time you have spent pursuing Jesus, worshiping Him, being in His Word, and cultivating your prayer life will benefit your marriage! All of these things will be immeasurable gifts you bring into the covenant relationship with your spouse. As you see God bring your dreams to life, you will know that it was *so worth the wait*. Even in my wedding vows to Sean, I told him that although I waited nineteen years for him, I would have waited nineteen more! Because when you wait on the Lord, He gives you His best!

Lastly, never lose sight that this is God writing your story, not you. He is the Author and Creator of all things, and your life is one He is giving His full attention to. You are blessed and highly favored, so live like the King's kid you are. You were born with a destiny and your best days are not behind you but ahead of you. Know that I am praying for you as you continue to walk your journey out. You are not alone in this. There are sisters and brothers cheering you on in the days ahead! You've got this, but even more importantly, God's got this!

Be blessed greatly and go live the life you were created to live!

ZERO IN ON:

➤ **You are a carrier of the message. Your convictions and pursuit of Jesus will encourage others around you.**

➤ **The gift of singleness is a message that the masses need. Marriage is not your goal, Jesus is.**

➤ **Never lose sight that this is God writing your story, not you.**

ADDENDUM

He is Abba, Almighty,

Advocate, Alpha and Omega,

Beginning and the End, Avenger,

Anointed One, Bridegroom,

Bright and Morning Star, Breath of Life,

Chosen One, Shepherd, Comforter,

Commander, Consuming Fire,

Cornerstone, Counselor, and Creator.

Deliverer and Door. He is Eternal,

Everlasting, All Consuming.

He is Judge, Righteousness,

Mercy. He is Truth,

All-Knowing, Ever-Present.

He is the Lion and Lamb. He is Life.

He is Light. He is Lily of the Valley.

He is Pure. He is True.

He is Glory, Master, Mediator,

Merciful God. He is Healer,

Restorer, Mighty One.

He is Shalom, Peace, Rest, and Joy.

The Way, The Living Word.

Faithful, Father, and Friend.

God Who Sees Me, Great Shepherd,

Great High Priest,

Guide, and Gentle Whisper,

God Over All. High Priest,

Holy One, Our Hope. Immanuel,

Jehovah-Jireh, Our Provider.

Potter, Prophet, Purifier. Teacher,

Redeemer, Refiner's Fire,

Righteous One, Resurrection, Rock,

Root of David, Rose of Sharon,

Ruler, Savior, Scepter, Seed, Servant,

Shepherd of our Souls, Shield,

Source, Stone, True Light.

Jehovah-Nissi, "The Lord our banner."

Jehovah-Shalom, "The Lord is peace."

EL-Shaddai, "God Almighty."

Jehovah-Rapha, "The Lord our Healer."

HE IS THE GREAT I AM.

HIS NAME IS JESUS!

ABOUT THE AUTHOR

Marriage is the number one desire of most people, yet so many of us have to wait for it to happen. Christa Smith is no exception. At nineteen years old, Christa prayed a prayer that set the tone for the next twenty years of her life. She asked God to take her heart, guard it, shield it, and give it back to her when she was to give it away. Little did she know she would be waiting till she was thirty-nine before that desire would become reality. The journey of relying on God and trusting Him with His timing for her life has been the foundation of Christa's relationship with Jesus. With over twenty-plus years in full-time ministry, Christa has trained up young adults in schools of ministry she has planted and has been passionate about a generation falling in love with Jesus. As an associate pastor, executive pastor, young adults pastor, and itinerant minister, Christa has always desired for people to pursue the call of God on their life regardless of their relationship status. She was determined to live fully for God whether she got married or not. In her free time, Christa loves home design and spending time with family and friends, and is a student of Krav Maga. In 2015, Christa married the love of her life, Sean, and they currently reside in the San Francisco Bay area. Sean and Christa travel together full-time, ministering and pouring into a generation hungry for the more of God.